Darlene,
Jesus Makes All Things New!
2 Cor 5:17
Deborah Barr

All Things New

All Things New

A Former Lesbian's Lifelong Search for Love

Debora Barr

All Things New: A Former Lesbian's Lifelong Search for Love

ISBN: 978-1-935769-32-3
UPC: 88571300076-5

Printed in the United States of America.

DBarrMinistries@gmail.com
www.DBarrMinistries.org

True Potential Publishing
PO Box 904
Travelers Rest, SC 29690

1 2 3 4 5 6 7 / 16 15 14 13

Dedication

This book is dedicated to my mother, whom I love dearly and whom God used to set in motion my life journey to discover the amazing love of Jesus.

I also dedicate this book to the women of Covenant Baptist Church, who loved me unconditionally and who helped me to heal when I didn't even know I was hurting.

Finally, I owe a great debt of gratitude to Clarise, my dear sister in Christ, who gently pushed me outside of my comfort zone years ago to begin sharing the testimony of what God has done in my life and who continues to pray for me and encourage me to this day.

Endorsements

Debora's testimony reveals the incredible power of Jesus Christ to transform lives. Her transparency and willingness to expose her heart for all to see as she recounts the path she took to apply the Word of God to her life will encourage you wherever you are in your walk with the Lord. This book is a must-read for churches interested in ministering to people from all walks of life. It contains a shining example of how the church should respond with the unconditional love of Christ toward all people.

Archbishop Alfred A. Owens, Jr.
Greater Mount Calvary Holy Church
Washington, DC

An engaging and provocative life story that sometimes makes you cry and later has you applauding for the triumphant victories in Debora's life. It is a celebration of finding and embracing what she had been searching for most of her life: true love, which is found in the arms of God. This is a now story for present-day problems that many people face daily in the secular world and in Christian society. This testimonial is brutally honest and revealing of the struggles of same-sex attraction yet gives us joy in the victory of God's power. It exemplifies Romans 8:37: "Nay, in all these things we are more than conquerors through him that loved us" (KJV*).*

Associate Pastor Ramona Moore
The Temple of Praise
Washington, D.C.

What a compelling, convicting and challenging testimony. The record of this writing is challenging to those who are participants in the struggle with same-sex attraction and yet is also challenging to those who are spectators standing on the sidelines with their Christian morals.

Debora has certainly demonstrated in the pages of this chronicle her odyssey of resurrection and transformation. It's obvious that such a transformation in Debora's life required a level of faith that could have easily been abandoned as a result of the religious misinformation that was imparted in her life. Her willingness to be transparent speaks volumes about her commitment to reach others with a transformative message of love. This book is a testament to what God can do and what agape love is all about. It's a must-read!

Senior Pastor Anthony E. Moore
Carolina Missionary Baptist Church
Fort Washington, Maryland

Christianity has often been delivered up in carefully choreographed, highly sanitized packages that many times leave us short of the real stuff of change. Debora Barr, however, delivers up a powerful and deeply personal revelation of her transition from a committed lesbian relationship to a single heterosexual woman committed to pleasing the Lord. You will marvel at her honesty and transparent portrayal of resounding highs and crashing lows in her journey. This book is for anyone who desires to transition away from any controlling life issue.

Pastor Ronald E. Crawford
New Vision Church
Bowie, Maryland

One of the greatest joys of my life has been watching the personal transformation of Debora Barr. Her spiritual journey will challenge those who believe they have fallen beyond the reach of God's grace, and her transparency about the painful struggle of living a holy life will encourage those wanting to love God with all their heart, soul, mind and strength.

Senior Pastor J. Scott Hesler
Potomac Baptist Church
Potomac Falls, Virginia

Debora Barr's story is both authentic and inspiring. And she shares it with a combination of transparency and compassion. Now that her story is in print, people all over the world can be moved by it.

Lead Pastor Keith Battle
Zion Church
Bowie, Maryland

ALL THINGS NEW is an amazing testament of God's power to heal. I am encouraged by Debora's story that displays God's endless love and ability to overcome any issue holding you back from His best for your life. This book is life-changing!

Senior Pastor Bobby Manning
First Baptist Church of District Heights
District Heights, Maryland

This book is a must-read for those who have questions about same-sex attraction and how a loving non-threatening environment can allow the word of God to have preeminence that leads to a relationship with Christ. Debora, thank you for your courage to be a source of illumination and enlightenment and for telling your story with such grace.

Pastor Louis B. Jones II
Pilgrim Baptist Church
Washington, D.C.

Debora Barr's autobiography, ALL THINGS NEW, offers an inspirational story of transformation. Debora allows us private glimpses into her heart and mind as she journeys from pain to prosperity. Anyone reading this book will be inspired by the amazing grace of God's redemptive love.

Richard Cohen, M.A., Author
Gay Children, Straight Parents
Coming Out Straight

Contents

Foreword

Everybody wants to feel loved. The yearning for love is in our DNA. We enter life demanding to be loved and cared for, and for most of us, those needs are met at home where we are surrounded by familial love. Then as we move into adolescence, we long to be found attractive and desirous. Intuitively, we seek the companionship of the opposite sex to satisfy our yearning for romantic love. Ultimately, we want total and complete acceptance. We want the assurance that we are loved—warts and all.

Our search for unconditional love is fulfilled in a personal relationship with Jesus Christ. He is the manifestation of God's unconditional and sacrificial love for mankind. The journey to experiencing the richness of God's love may take us down many roads. If our needs for familial love and romantic love go unmet or are somehow distorted, we may find ourselves looking for love in all the wrong places. Love unfulfilled can be a dangerous thing. Feelings of dejection and desperation can cause us to compromise what we know to be true and leave us vulnerable. Instead of holding out for true love and acceptance, we settle for abusive, dysfunctional and ungodly relationships.

Ask Debora Barr. She knows all too well where unmet needs can lead. Having grown up in a broken home and having fallen victim to inappropriate sexual advances, she did not know what real love looked like. Confused, lonely and longing for love, she found solace in the arms of another woman. Her experimentation with lesbianism led to a same-sex lifestyle and, ultimately, to a civil union with a woman lover. It took the love of a God-fearing church family to open her eyes to the true meaning of love. Their love, tolerance, prayers, biblical instruction, gentle rebuke, godly wisdom and patience won Debora to the Lord. Having a relationship with Him and experiencing His love transformed her life.

Debora's story is not uncommon. The number of men and women turning to homosexuality is alarming. Society would have us accept homosexuality as the norm, legitimize same-sex relationships and ostracize anyone who speaks out against gay rights. What I love about Debora's story is that she does not involve the reader in the social discourse and controversy of same-sex relationships. She goes straight to the heart of the matter and removes all stigma, judgment and condemnation. Her personal account of what drew her to a lifestyle of homosexuality and what led her out of it allows us to see the person behind the label. She brings us face to face with the reality that we are all capable of wandering away from God and, no matter what form of sin we choose to engage in, that He is calling us back to a relationship with Him. It is the ultimate love story—a story of God's redeeming love.

I thank God for giving Debora the courage to share her story with us. Her transparency is refreshing. Her transformation is miraculous. Her testimony is enlightening. If you have ever discounted God or professed Christianity, this book is for you. Read it and witness God's love in action.

May the sweet love of Jesus enrapture you as it has Debora.

Enjoy!

First Lady Trina Jenkins
Women's Ministry Director
First Baptist Church of Glenarden, Maryland

All Things New

A Former Lesbian's Lifelong Search for Love

CHAPTER 1

My Early Years
(1963–1976)

When I was a child, I spoke as a child, I understood as a child, I thought as a child; but when I became a [wo]man, I put away childish things.

1 CORINTHIANS 13:11

I have overcome the bondage imposed by the enemy of my soul by the precious blood of Jesus Christ and by the word of my testimony (Rev. 12:11)! I will never stop proclaiming the riches of God's glory available to all through the power of His Spirit, to those who allow Jesus Christ to dwell in their heart through faith, enabling them to be rooted and grounded in love and capable of comprehending the width and length and depth and height of His love for them (Eph. 3:16-19).

For most of my forty-eight years on this earth I was lord and master of my life. I was extremely selfish and self-sufficient and I worked hard to achieve status and recognition in all areas of my life. I have had an amazing professional career, flying helicopters for the U.S. Army and for the National Oceanic and Atmospheric Administration (NOAA). I have worked directly for generals and admirals and have traveled to many places in the world. I have seen incredible places and things like magnificent castles in the countryside of Germany and camels running in the deserts of the Middle East; I've explored caves in the Midwestern United States; I have seen polar bears, whales and other magnificent creatures in the wild on the north slope of Alaska and the Bering Sea; I have observed humpback whales breaching near the Galapagos Islands; and I have seen blue whales up close in the middle of the Pacific Ocean. However, even with all of that, I sensed an aching void in my heart that just could not be satisfied. I didn't know what my purpose was, but God began to stir my spirit and draw me to Him. I realized that all of the incredible things I had experienced could not fill the void in my heart. In 2003, the pastor of the church I was attending challenged the congregation to "40 Days of Purpose," where we collectively worked through *The Purpose Driven Life* by Rick Warren. I found that what was missing in my life was a personal relationship with Jesus Christ.

It Was Jesus!

I accepted Jesus as my Lord and Savior and was born again, and my life changed forever! Since then Jesus has completely filled that void in my heart with His unconditional and pure love. I realized that I had been separated from God for a very long time. When I was in control of my life I was sinning against God, and the penalty for my sin was separation from Him (Rom. 3:23). Jesus Christ died on the cross to take away my sins and offered to me His free gift of salvation (Rom. 6:23). All I had to do was admit that I was a sinner, believe that Jesus died for my sins and ask for His forgiveness. I did. I asked Him to take over as Lord and Savior of my life and I gave up the role that I held for so long. I started to focus on the things that matter to God and miracles began to occur in my life. It was as if He rearranged my very DNA. Everything about my life has changed! He changed the way I think, the way I act and the way I react. Now I am living my life with full satisfaction and purpose. All things are new!

IT WAS AS IF GOD REARRANGED MY VERY DNA. EVERYTHING ABOUT MY LIFE HAS CHANGED!

As I began to study the Word of God, I found the story of my life right there in the pages of the Bible. When I dug deeper into the Word, I became more and more excited about life as I developed an intimate relationship with Jesus, the lover of my soul. As a result, my life was being completely transformed. I hope that my testimony will encourage you to see how God has worked in my life and that you will realize that God is no respecter of persons. He does not show partiality for one person over another (Acts 10:34). The incredible miracles that God performed in the lives of Moses, Abraham, Joseph, Paul and Debora Barr, He can and will do for you if you surrender your life to Him and love Him with all of your heart!

Much of the content of this book comes directly from my journal and emails that I sent to friends. Many of these entries and messages contain my written prayers and conversations with God. Each journal entry or email is preceded by the date of the entry, and for the sake of this book been edited to correct mistakes. I also changed many of the names of people in my life to protect their identities.

What follows is God's story of my life. It is my story of transformation and I hope it blesses you. If you don't yet know Jesus as your personal Lord and Savior, I pray that you too will surrender your life to Him and let Him take control of every area of your life. You will never be the same!

My Beginning

I came into this world in December of 1963, the daughter of young parents who each had difficult childhoods, and the oldest of four children. Both of my parents came from homes where a parent died when they were still children. My dad was an only child and his father died when he was just ten years old. Likewise, my mom's mother died when she was ten years old. She was only sixteen years old when she married my dad to get away from her alcoholic father and the responsibilities of raising her two younger brothers.

I knew and loved God as a little girl. My mother took me to Catholic Church every week where I learned about God, Jesus and religion. My understanding of who God is was very different at that time in my life. I remember one Sunday afternoon I had a plan that I just knew would work because I believed God would perform a miracle for me. Going into my bedroom, I closed the door and put a plastic model horse in the middle of the room. I then moved other things out of the way and began to pray to God that He would turn it into a real horse because I loved horses and wanted one of my own. Looking back on that incident, I am glad God didn't answer that prayer because I have no idea how I would have gotten that horse out of the house or where I would have kept him if God had answered that prayer!

When I was growing up, I was very insecure and did not make friends easily. I had trouble connecting with kids my own age and usually had one or two older friends whom I connected with. For as long as I can remember, I have been competitive and achievement-oriented, striving to excel in everything I got involved in. I was also very much a tomboy growing up. One day when I was quite young, my mother dropped me off at a neighbor's house for dance lessons and I cried the entire time I was there because I was so shy and didn't want to participate in any of the dancing lessons. My mom never took me back. Instead I played softball and was very involved in music, playing the clarinet in the orchestra and marching band and playing the piano for many years. I was also driven academically and excelled in school, especially in science. In elementary school, I had already decided on a future career as a doctor and was working toward that. Little did I know that my life would not follow the plan I had envisioned.

LITTLE DID I KNOW THAT MY LIFE WOULD NOT FOLLOW THE PLAN I HAD ENVISIONED.

In sixth grade I began to exhibit signs of stress in my life: I started compulsively pulling out my hair, which left embarrassing bald spots on my head. I now know that this disorder is called trichotillomania. I ended up struggling with that disorder for about fifteen years. When it started, I was babysitting a lot for my younger brothers and sister and the foster children my family took in at the time. We would usually have two infants at a time in foster care. So much responsibility in addition to my self-imposed pressure to excel at school, music and sports was beginning to take its toll on me.

CHAPTER 2

The Difficult Years
(1977–1987)

There is a way that seems right to a man,
but its end is the way of death.

PROVERBS 14:12

My family moved to a new neighborhood in 1977, which meant I moved to a new school district just prior to entering the seventh grade. I had a lot of trouble making friends in this new school and was bullied by girls in the band who threatened me because I was competing for the first chair position for clarinet. I really didn't feel welcome in this new school, plus I had very low self-esteem.

In the summer of 1978, I went to summer band camp and met an older guy who I really liked and who had similar goals for his future. (We both wanted to be doctors.) John and I began dating. I was fifteen years old when I met him and we dated for a couple of years. During the weekends, we would go to movies, go bowling, play billiards and hang out at my house.

My mom would spend a lot of time with John and me and the three of us would sometimes do things together. I was very close to my mother during this time in my life and considered her to be my best friend.

John began to make sexual advances toward me. He tried many times to pressure me into sexual activity every time we were alone together, and I was very uncomfortable with his advances so I ended up breaking off my relationship with him. Around the same time, I experienced deep betrayal from someone very close to me, which altered the course of my life forever. This resulted in my diving headlong into depression. all of this happened in 1980 when I was in tenth grade.

Angry, Depressed and Suicidal

I got angry with God and completely turned my back on Him, denying that He even existed. I allowed Satan to convince me that what I knew of God as a child was a lie; that if God were real, He would have never allowed this turn of events in my life. I fully embraced the lie that religion and the existence of God was a figment of people's imagination—there was no God! I was so depressed that I entertained the thought of suicide on more than one occasion and planned out how I would kill myself. I began taking drugs and secretly drinking hard alcohol to numb the pain. I even got into the car one evening with the full intent of driving at a high rate of speed into a tree to kill myself. As I accelerated toward the tree, I saw a vision of the four-year-old foster child, who I loved as if he were my own child, crawling across the road in front of me, and I slammed on the brakes to avoid hitting him. Little did I know that the God I was denying was watching over me and protecting me even in my rebellion toward Him.

I FULLY EMBRACED THE LIE THAT THERE WAS NO GOD.

As soon as I graduated from high school and headed to college my parents divorced. My father moved halfway across the country and took my brothers and sister to live with him. I ended up breaking off my relationship with both of my parents. They both got remarried to other people, and our family was broken, never to recover. I went to college rejecting the dream of becoming a doctor because I didn't want anything to do with John and the dreams we had planned together. I paid my way through college by working multiple jobs while going to school full-time. In my first year of college I met a girl named Jackie and she and I became friends instantly. In fact, we became roommates and did everything together. I stayed with her family during the summer breaks because I didn't have a family or place to go home to. Jackie was majoring in geology, so I ended up switching my major from biology to geology.

It was in my first year of college that I was sexually assaulted the first time. One of my employers began to take special notice of me and requested that I wear nice clothes to my job at the donut shop where I worked. I was completely naïve and did what he requested. Late one night he cornered me in the back room and tried to force me to have sex with him. I managed to break away from him and never went back to that job. I experienced two more similar incidents involving older men during my first two years of college.

Smoking and Sharing a Bed

To discourage men from noticing me I began to dress and act in an asexual manner. I wanted to protect myself from the negative attention I was receiving from them. I continued to struggle with self-esteem issues and the hair-pulling disorder along with bouts of depression. I also began smoking and was soon smoking more than two packs of cigarettes a day. Jackie was my only friend and I completely depended on her for comfort and affirmation. Toward everyone else, I had built a wall of stone around my heart for protection.

At some point in college, Jackie and I began to sleep together. I don't know how or why it started, but it was not a sexual relationship. I think we did it solely for the comfort of human touch and companionship. Eventually she began dating a guy who moved into our house and I had to endure the emotional pain of losing her intimacy and hearing them together in the next room. I was extremely jealous and began to wonder about my sexuality. This greatly exacerbated my depression, hair-pulling disorder and chain-smoking. At twenty-one years of age, I sought counseling from a psychologist who suggested that I was a lesbian. He told me to stop fighting it and accept who I was. I rejected his diagnosis and never went back to him.

"Stop fighting it and accept who you are."

I graduated from college with a degree in geology but couldn't find a job as a geologist. I then decided to go to graduate school but didn't do well on the entrance exam for the master's program at the school I had just graduated from, so I slid further into depression. I ended up working at a factory that made television cabinets. I was miserable! I was paying off student loans and working in a factory. The child who dreamed of being a doctor, who had excelled at school her whole life, was working beside people on an assembly line who never seemed to aspire to do anything more than add their piece to the television cabinet, collect their paycheck and go home. Then one day in 1987, on the way to my factory job, I saw a helicopter sitting in a field and immediately thought it would be awesome to fly a helicopter (even though I had never left the ground in a helicopter or an airplane my whole life). I visited a couple of military recruiters to inquire about flying helicopters and shortly thereafter joined the U.S. Army.

CHAPTER 3

The Tumultuous Years

(1988–1999)

But your iniquities have separated you from your God; and your sins have hidden His face from you, so that He will not hear.

Isaiah 59:2

In the Army

There I was, twenty-four years old and in basic training for the Army. I was chosen to be the platoon sergeant since I was six years older than all of the other recruits (my fellow recruits called me grandma). Once again I began to excel in this competitive environment, graduating at the top of my class in basic training and in Warrant Officer training. I then entered helicopter flight school and there I met a woman who would change the course of the next eighteen years of my life. She kissed me and gently introduced me to homosexuality. As a result, she ended up being my first lesbian lover, and I fell head over heels in love with her.

At first, I was repelled and disgusted with myself for kissing a woman. Somewhere deep inside I knew it was wrong and went completely against nature, but I was so starved for love, compassion and touch that I suppressed the uncomfortable feelings and succumbed to her advances. Here we were, two women in a male-dominated profession, and I had found someone who understood me and could relate to me. We were deeply secretive of our relationship. She broke my heart over and over again because she was still involved with another woman when she seduced me and would go back and forth between us. Early on I even tried to run from homosexuality by succumbing to the sexual advances of a couple of different married men. I was trying to figure out who I was, but in the end I went back to my lesbian lover.

I didn't know this at the time, but I have since learned that there are several predictable root causes for same-sex attraction. Many women who experience same-sex attraction like myself have had broken relationships with their mothers at some stage during their development. For me, my relationship with my mother was severed before I became an adult. The mother-daughter relationship is very important for the proper sexual development of a woman. Another factor in the development of my own same-sex attraction was the sexual assault and inappropriate advances that I experienced from men. I determined from experience that it was not safe to have any kind of intimate relationship with men. A third factor for me, and I hear this from other women who have experienced same-sex attraction, is that I always felt different from other females, even from my earliest memories, like I really didn't fit in. I never had a healthy group of friends around me. I was mostly a loner and tried desperately to gain attention, recognition and love by excelling in everything I did.

In 1989 I graduated from flight school and was sent overseas to Germany. This was the first time I had ever been outside of the United States, and I was definitely like a fish out of water. I didn't speak the language and had a tough time finding my way around. A couple of months after I got to Germany, my lesbian partner also arrived in Germany and we were stationed in the same military unit. We continued our roller-coaster relationship deep in the closet over the next several years.

While in Germany, I reestablished contact with a woman I had known since I was about eight years old. Mary was my third grade teacher and we had been pen pals for many years following her exit from teaching in 1972. She became like a second mom to me after my relationship with my mother was severed. Mary and I checked in with each other periodically, and she even came to Germany to visit me. Little did I know it at the time, but the relationship that God allowed to start when I was in the third grade would be a stabilizing factor in my life many years later as Mary became family to me.

GOD COVERED AND PROTECTED ME EVEN WHEN I WAS STAYING SO FAR AWAY FROM HIM.

In December of 1990, my lesbian partner and I were deployed to the Middle East for Desert Storm where we experienced war together as we spent five months in Saudi Arabia, Iraq and Kuwait. I remember one particularly bad argument we had with each other while in the war zone. My emotions during this relationship were extreme. She threatened to break up with me and I was so distraught that I wandered around in a minefield in the dark of night not caring whether I lived or died. But God cared. He covered and protected me even when I was staying so far away from Him.

In 1992, it was time for me to rotate to my next military assignment. I was sent to Fort Campbell, Kentucky. My partner also received orders to go to Fort Campbell, but she managed to get her duty station changed because she wanted to sever ties with me. I guess I had become too clingy and she wanted to move on without me. I moved back to the States and slipped into my deepest depression yet. I literally thought I would die from grief.

Mary realized how sick I was becoming as I continued to grieve over the next several months, so she invited me to come to Atlanta to visit her. I went several times on the weekends since it was driving distance from where I lived. These visits helped lift me out of my depression and brought me healing. Soon thereafter, I began traveling and often frequented gay bars to try to meet other people and to get my mind off my first failed relationship. I ended up meeting another woman and the two of us began a long-distance relationship; this woman lived in Mississippi and I lived in Kentucky. I was completely out of the closet in this relationship (in my private life outside of the military, that is). I was proud to be a lesbian and no longer wanted to hide who I was.

In the late summer of 1992, I was on a military flight on the way to Honduras when I began talking to a fellow pilot about wanting to do something different with my life. He told me about the possibility of flying helicopters for the National Oceanic and Atmospheric Administration (NOAA) where I could fly scientific research missions. I was intrigued, and after returning to Fort Campbell, did some research on NOAA. In the summer of 1993, at the age of thirty, I left the Army and joined NOAA.

Flying for the NOAA

When I started with NOAA, I was initially stationed in Florida, where I moved in with the parents of my lesbian partner who lived in Mississippi. Not long after I moved in with her parents, she dumped me. A few months later I met another woman named Jennifer and entered into a relationship with her. I also bought my first house and began to settle down. God uniquely used this woman to begin to draw me back to Him. Remember, at this time in my life I still didn't believe that God existed; in fact, I had become an atheist over these many years. I had solidified in my scientific mind, full of scientific education, that the Bible was a lie and that there was no God. Whenever a person mentioned God or religion, I would tell that person that he or she was deluding him or herself; that by believing in an invisible God he or she was only fooling him or herself.

One day in 1994, when I was dating Jennifer, she asked me to go to church with her. I immediately stated that I didn't believe in God and hadn't crossed the threshold of a church in nearly fifteen years. At that time in my life I thought that people who believed in God were weak and deluded because I was unable to discern spiritual things. The Bible says, "The natural man does not receive the things of the Spirit of God, for they are foolishness to him; nor can he know them, because they are spiritually discerned" (1 Cor. 2:14). What she said to me, however, began to change the course of my life. She looked me right in the eyes and said, "Jesus wants you back." There was something in her sincerity that penetrated my soul and began to bore a hole in the thick wall of stone that I had built around my heart, and I personally experienced what the Bible says: "I will give you a new heart and put a new spirit within you; I will take the heart of stone out of your flesh and give you a heart of flesh. I will put My Spirit within you and cause you to walk in My statutes, and you will keep My judgments and do them" (Ezek. 36:26-27).

"JESUS WANTS YOU BACK."

I agreed to go to church with her and began attending a Metropolitan Community Church (MCC) full of same-sex couples. The pastor was in a committed same-sex relationship and there I was taught that sexuality is a holy gift from God; therefore, I was living perfectly within the will of God for my life. It was very different from the Catholic Church I grew up in. I was taught pro-gay theology at MCC and was fully equipped to refute anybody who said the Bible does not condone homosexuality. I was taught that scripture passages in the Bible that cast homosexuality in a negative light, such as Leviticus 20:13, Romans 1:26-27 and First Corinthians 6:9, don't really mean what they say and that particular words and concepts in these passages were mistranslated over the years. The pastor taught me everything I needed to know and I never investigated the Word of God on my own.

I began to settle into my life in Florida. I was back in church after a great number of years away; was working on renovating my house (built in 1917); and traveling a lot for my job. It was during my relationship with Jennifer, and after I joined the gay church, that I finally "came out" to my family. On December 18, 1994, I videotaped my neighborhood and my new home, and near the end of the tape I sat down in the living room, looked into the camera and said:

> *"I want you to know that I am gay. I am very happy with myself and I am very happy with my lifestyle. I am not saying this to hurt you. I want to be closer to you. I want you to know who I am. I want to be honest with you. I would like you to meet my partner* [Jennifer moves into the frame]. *We are very happy together. We've got a good life together. I would like for you to meet her someday. Please don't be angry with me. Like I said, I am not saying this to hurt you. I love you."*

I mailed one copy of that tape to my mother and another copy to my father and then waited nervously for a response. I can't really explain it, but deep down inside I needed affirmation from my parents even though our family had been ripped apart twelve years earlier. At that time in my life, I rarely communicated with my parents, only speaking to them about once or twice a year. I don't remember exactly how it transpired, but I was not rejected by either of them. In the end nervousness gave way to relief.

Over time my relationship with Jennifer began to deteriorate. She began abusing alcohol and painkillers and was emotionally and sexually abusive toward me. I had to travel a lot for work and she would take care of my German Shepherd for a month at a time while I was traveling. Often times she would get drunk and call me when I was out of town or out of the country. She accused me of loving the dog more than her and threatened to get rid of him while I was away. Needless to say, it created a lot of stress for me as I tried to focus on my job not knowing what she was doing at home.

In 1998 I had a very close call while flying. I was flying a small helicopter off of the back of a NOAA research ship in the Pacific Ocean. As I was preparing to lift off from the back deck of the ship with two scientists aboard the helicopter, the tail rotor drive shaft separated from the engine. If it had been just a few seconds later in the takeoff procedure, the results could have been devastating. As it turned out, nobody got hurt but it really shook me up. Once again God protected me from harm, knowing that soon I would come to know and love Him. God is extremely patient and oh so forgiving, even when we, His children, take the wrong path while seeking Him!

Searching for God

Around this same time, I was still wondering about God and why I was here, so I began reading the series of books entitled *Conversations With God: An Uncommon Dialogue* by Neale Donald Walsch. I didn't know at the time that what is written in those books is not biblically sound. I was absorbing the New Age thinking that the books portray, which further validated and endorsed the life I was living as a lesbian. Another book I read was *The Origin* by Irving Stone, which is about Charles Darwin and his struggle of trying to reconcile his faith with the natural world around him and his scientific knowledge. I could relate to Charles Darwin because I too was a scientist and had been taught the timeline of geologic processes, which did not line up with what the Bible says about the earth and time.

Another avenue I took in the pursuit of my life's purpose was to attend personal development seminars hosted by Landmark Education LLC. This represented more "New Age" thinking that taught me that I could create my own meaning for life and that I could transform my life by declaring a new way of being instead of trying to change myself in comparison to the past. My personal transformation statement was, "I am the possibility of peace, power and integrity." One significant thing that I accomplished during one of the Landmark seminars was the complete forgiveness of the person who betrayed me when I was a teenager. That was a powerful moment in my life! It really helped further break down the thick walls I had constructed around my heart. It definitely contributed to my healing.

God was actually pursuing me!

During this period in my life, I was seeking God and trying to understand who He was, who I was and why I was here. Little did I know that He was actually pursuing me! Only much later was I able to recognize that everything I have experienced in my life ultimately has been used to glorify God; that He has been watching over me all of my life, even when I turned my back on Him and denied His existence. He has even allowed me to experience false teachings about Him so I can help others avoid my mistakes. "And we know that all things work together for good to those who love God, to those who are the called according to His purpose" (Rom. 8:28).

By late 1999, my home life was miserable. I discovered that my lesbian partner of six years was cheating on me. To make matters worse, Cindy, the partner of the woman whom Jennifer was seeing, began to pursue a relationship with me. Cindy and I, both jilted by our lovers, started a relationship with each other, which I knew would not continue for long. My life was in great turmoil. In addition to the stressful relationship issues, I was about to be transferred from Florida to Washington, D.C., for my job and was trying to sell my house. I also had made plans to spend Thanksgiving with my mother, whom I hadn't talked to in some time, but I had to cancel those plans to unexpectedly go back to the ship and fly the helicopter once again.

I then had an amazing encounter with God, who I had been trying to get to know. Following is part of my journal entry for November 2, 1999:

> *I was walking at Crescent Lake Park and praying to God for increased and strengthened faith when He spoke to me loud and clear for the first time I can recall without a doubt. He said to me, "Sit, child...rest, and know that I am God."*

I clearly remember that day. I was feeling sorry for myself and walking my dog around the lake when I heard what I thought was a loud booming voice. I immediately looked behind me and then at my dog to see if he had heard what I heard, but apparently I was the only one who heard it. I was so startled that I sat under a tree for the longest time pondering what had just happened. Some months later, I either read or heard the following scripture verse for the very first time: "Be still, and know that I am God" (Ps. 46:10a). He was trying to get my attention!

CHAPTER 4

The Transition Years

(2000–2005)

Part I

If My people who are called by My name
will humble themselves, and pray and seek My face, and turn
from their wicked ways, then I will hear from heaven,
and will forgive their sin and heal their land.

2 CHRONICLES 7:14

Six weeks later I was driving a moving truck from Florida to Washington, D.C., to begin a new job and a new chapter in my life. I was leaving my relationship troubles behind; the woes from my relationship with Jennifer and my short-term relationship with Cindy were about to be over.

I found a lesbian realtor and began looking for a place to live in a gay community where I would feel welcome. While looking for a house, I experienced sticker shock at the cost of housing in and around D.C.

compared to where I had moved from. So I ended up buying a house in West Virginia, where I could buy a much larger house for the money. It was a long way away from where I worked, but there was a commuter train that made the trip feasible. Once I got settled in my new home, I started looking for a local MCC church to attend.

The closest MCC church was about a forty minute drive from my house and I began to connect with the local gay community. There I discovered that there was an active lesbian group even closer to my home that met regularly for dinner and get-togethers. I was invited to attend a party and met Barb, my next lesbian partner, on April 22, 2000. About two months later, she moved in with me (if you don't already know, it is kind of a joke with lesbians that on the second date one woman brings the U-Haul to move in with the other). We began looking for property to build a house together since she didn't want to live long-term in my house, and her house was up for sale. That summer she and I sold our individual properties (my house in Florida and my house in West Virginia, and her house and property in West Virginia), purchased land together and began to build our dream home, a beautiful custom-built log home on seven acres.

This relationship seemed different from all of my prior relationships. Barb is about ten years older than I am, and we were very compatible and settled in nicely together. We became very active in the gay community and were part of a "family" of lesbian women who were in committed long-term relationships. One year later on our anniversary, April 22, 2001, we went to Vermont to enter into a civil union (a legal relationship similar to marriage) to solidify our commitment to one another. When we returned to West Virginia, our house was nearing completion and we celebrated with our new friends and family.

A Church with Unconditional Love

By late 2001, I felt a strong pull from God to find another church and resume pursuing Him. I had stopped going to the MCC church that I found when I first moved to West Virginia because it wasn't like my church in Florida and I really didn't like it. I told Barb I wanted to go back to church, so she and I visited several of the churches in our small town. One Sunday, we decided to go to a relatively large church and found that we liked it very much. I expressed my concern to Barb as we drove out of the parking lot that first day when I saw for the first time the sign that indicated the church was a Baptist church. I was worried that they would not accept us as a lesbian couple in this church because I had been taught by the MCC church to be highly suspicious of mainstream Christian denominations such as Baptists. I had been taught to view them as homophobic. However, we were drawn back to that church Sunday after Sunday by the friendliness of the people, the energetic praise and worship music and the message that was being taught from the Bible in a way we could understand. We soon made a decision that we would not try to hide our relationship with each other and that we would continue to go to that church. We felt that we would eventually bring change to the church regarding their views on homosexuality. We were convinced that when the leaders of the church got to know us and saw how we had such a pure love for each other, that they would eventually accept gays and lesbians openly.

In 2003, Barb and I tried to join the church as a couple. However, we were not allowed to become members of the church if we insisted on signing up together. At the same time, we experienced love in our dealings with the various pastors and elders who spoke to us, and we were gently counseled by each of them about the Bible and what it says about homosexuality. In love, they each told us that they did not agree with our choice of lifestyle but that we were welcome to continue to attend church there; however, we could not become members of the church while continuing to openly live in the sin of homosexuality.

Later that year, our pastor challenged the whole church to "40 Days of Purpose" as we worked in small groups to read *The Purpose Driven Life* by Rick Warren. It was during my study of that book and the accompanying scriptures that I yielded my heart to Jesus and accepted Him as Lord and Savior of my life. I fully understood for the first time all that Jesus had done for me in dying on the cross for my sins. I repented, asked for forgiveness and invited the Lord to take over my life. The amazing thing I now realize is that everything I had experienced up to this point in my life—the people I met along the way; the good and bad things I had experienced—everything had a purpose in God's perfect plan for my life. He had been watching over me and trying to get my attention over and over, and now He truly had my heart. (See Jeremiah 29:11-13.)

At the end of the forty days, our church planned a Sunday evening celebration service where we could be baptized. I immediately signed up to be baptized, and so did Barb. The day before this celebration service, we received a phone call at our home asking us to meet with the associate pastor following church service the next morning. We went to his office the next day not knowing what the meeting was about. What we quickly discovered was that he was going to confront us about our homosexuality. He said he didn't think he could baptize us because we were openly living in sin. We talked for a long time and told him how much we loved Jesus and that we were seeking God's will for our lives. We believed that God put us together, and our love for each other didn't seem wrong to us. We told him that if God revealed to us that we were living in sin we would immediately repent and turn away from that sin. In the end, he decided to allow us to be baptized that evening.

Here is my journal entry from that evening (November 23, 2003):

I am so thankful that Jesus lives in me and that I made my commitment to serve Him for eternity. God, thank You for loving me and filling my soul with Your Holy Spirit. I pray that I will serve You proudly and that You will continue to live in me and guide my actions and feelings the rest of the days I have on this earth. I vow to continue to study Your Word and learn more about You and how You want me to live my life every day. Jesus, give me the courage and wisdom to share Your good news with all people You want me to touch. Help me to look past my fears and step out for You. Praise God! Lord, teach me to love like You love—teach me not to judge, but to accept all of Your children as You accept and love them. Teach me to be unselfish in the sharing of my talents and time as You teach us in the Bible. Teach me to understand, comprehend and internalize Your Word in my life. God, I thank You for my church and for Pastor Mike and our conversation this morning about our lifestyle and our willingness to join the church. God, even though they don't approve of our lifestyle, we are accepted into the family. I pray that if it is Your will, Lord, we have an opportunity to create revolutionary change in this church and their beliefs about homosexuals. Thank You, God, for accepting us into this church family—we are at home here!

WHEN I WAS BAPTIZED, THE LORD PLANTED A SEED IN MY SOUL THAT WOULD FOREVER ALTER THE COURSE OF MY DESTINY.

I believe in my heart that when I was baptized, the Lord planted a seed in my soul that would forever alter the course of my destiny. "Therefore say to them, 'Thus says the LORD of hosts: "Return to Me," says the LORD of hosts, "and I will return to you," says the LORD of hosts'"

(Zech. 1:3). Around that same time, I began volunteering at the church to assist with the Sunday morning services and started getting involved in women's ministry. I wanted more and more to be around godly people who could speak into my life and teach me about my new life as a born-again Christian.

In the winter of 2004, Barb signed up for a women's small group at our church called "The Women Who Worship God." They were studying *The Power of a Praying Woman* by Stormie Omartian. Barb convinced me to start attending these sessions with her in the early part of 2005. We began to learn from Clarise, the women's ministry leader, how to fall in love with Jesus. Her enthusiasm for the Lord and her love for Him was unlike anything I had ever experienced. She truly loved the women in her group and had a special way of living out the love of Jesus in our presence.

Clarise was teaching us to love the Lord and to trust Him. Barb and I started to read the Bible together every day in the morning and again in the evening without fail. We began to get to know God in a personal and intimate way through His Word and were strengthened weekly by our participation in the women's group. It was in that women's group that I learned how to praise God and how to pray. I started praying that God would reveal His truth to me about my life. I also developed a love for the Word of God, which is where the *real* transformation in my life began to occur.

As Barb and I read the Bible together, we came across passages about homosexuality. Barb expressed concern and questioned me about what the Scriptures appeared to reveal about the impropriety of homosexuality. I was not concerned because I had been thoroughly indoctrinated in gay theology and was completely convinced that the Scriptures did not mean what they appeared to be saying. I responded to her concerns with what I believed to be the "real truth" about homosexuality, which I had been taught at MCC.

But it was God's plan in the end that I would come to know *the* Truth as I learned to rightly divide the Word of God (2 Tim. 2:15).

I experimented with applying what I was learning from the Bible to my life and was amazed at the transformation that began to occur in me. All the time (unbeknownst to Barb and me) the women's ministry leaders at the church loved us unconditionally, never once directly confronted us about how we were living, and prayed fervently (twice a day for months) for God to reveal His Truth to us. Around the same time He was revealing Himself to me, God began to open up new opportunities in another area of my life.

Around this time in my professional career, I was attending training classes at the University of Southern California where I took a course entitled Legal Aspects of Aviation Safety. The instructor of that class had been in the military, and later went to law school and became a lawyer. I was very intrigued by his career path, and something deep in my spirit began to stir. I started to think about becoming a lawyer.

On My Way to Becoming a Lawyer

In January 2005, I approached my boss to inquire about the possibility of going to law school and having NOAA pay my way. I had it all planned out: when I would take the Law School Aptitude Test (LSAT); when I would enter law school; and what career path I would follow upon my return to NOAA after the law school assignment. My boss told me that if I passed the LSAT and was accepted into a law school, he would do what he could to ensure I got into the Full-time University Training (FUT) assignment. On February 3, 2005, I submitted my formal request in writing to the NOAA Commissioned Personnel Center requesting a FUT assignment. Shortly thereafter, I began diligently studying for the LSAT.

In March, Clarise challenged me to join the women's praise dance group that she was forming to learn a dance to the song entitled "Shake

Yourself Loose" by Vickie Winans. I was so fearful because the thought of dancing brought back all of those memories from my five-year-old little girl body who was terrified to dance. Clarise was so gentle with me and continued to encourage me that I eventually pushed past my fear and danced with the group. I was so blessed by the power of God that I felt flooding through my whole body when I praised Him through dance that I couldn't get enough of it. The power was not only in the liberation of the dance, but also in the lyrics of the song, which encouraged me to "shake loose" what had bound me for so many years (the fear of dancing).

On April 28, 2005, I wrote the following email to Clarise:

Please pray for me. I am experiencing sciatic nerve pain that is progressively getting worse and I know that this is the enemy's attempt to prevent me from dancing on Saturday—but no matter what, I will dance!

I want to share with you a personal story related to dancing and how important it is to me that I participate this Saturday:

When I was in elementary school, my mother tried to take me to dance lessons. I was extremely shy and insecure and threw such a fit that she never took me back. For the next 35+ years, I watched from the sidelines as other people enjoyed themselves on the dance floor. I longed to participate, but when invited to, felt those insecurities rise rapidly to the surface and completely paralyze me.

When you first presented the idea of our group doing this dance, it terrified me, and I almost talked myself out of showing up on the Wednesday evening that I learned the dance.

When I did manage to get up the courage to show up, what did I see before we started but Cindy's little girl holding tightly to her mother's leg and screaming just as I did over 35 years ago! GOD tugged at my heart and revealed to me that I was no longer bound by the fear and insecurities of a little girl and that I can dance! I dance for the LORD!

This song and this dance represent a turning point in my life! Thank you for creating a safe environment for me to learn to worship through dance.

On April 30, 2005, I danced publicly for first time and then wrote the following in my journal:

Father, today I danced for You! Thank You for taking the shackles off my feet so I could dance in praise and worship to You, Father God. I feel free—free of my insecurities and free of everything that tied me down and kept me from being able to praise and worship You freely. Thank You for the incredible people You placed in my path to teach me and create a safe environment full of love and support so I could learn to dance. Father, I will always dance and praise You for You are worthy of all my praise! I love You, Jesus!

Today is a new day—a turning point in my life everlasting. Thank You for loving me and gently pulling me closer to You; I seek to know You more. I want to be in Your presence always, for You created me to worship You and worship You I do! Father, teach me Your ways. Empty me of myself and fill me up with Your love and blessings overflowing. Make me an instrument of Your peace and love everlasting; teach me to bring others to Your house. I sit and wait for You; You told me to be still and know that You are God. Help me always to be still and listen for Your presence. Teach me, mold me, love me and fill me with Your Holy Spirit—my counselor who guides me. Praise Jesus! I am Yours, Lord!

I continued to apply the Word of God to my life as I read and studied the Bible every day. I was falling in love with Jesus and falling in love with His Word.

On May 6, 2005, I sent another email to Clarise:

I know you already know this, but as a teacher and leader, I want to share with you some baby steps that are a direct result of breaking the shackles and trusting GOD completely through praise and worship.

I have known the power of GOD for quite some time—but kept it a secret that I only shared with a few very close friends and loved ones out of fear…fear of what others would think of me.

I am a commissioned officer in a uniformed service and probably appear outwardly to most people to personify the most common stereotypes of a commissioned officer (rigid, unfeeling, etc.). There is a lady in my office who absolutely drives me crazy with her whining and great drama about all of the tragedies of her life—which she lives out every day publicly for all to see. I used to avoid her at all costs when she was going through yet another tragedy for which she was seeking a shoulder to cry on.

I was falling in love with Jesus.

Well, that was until God asked me to go over and talk to her! I successfully avoided the first encounter on Tuesday evening when I was pretty sure it was her sitting on the bench to catch the train back home. (I made a lame excuse to God and claimed that I wasn't sure it was her, and if it was, I didn't have time to deal with her; I just wanted to get home.)

Well, opportunity number two hit me square yesterday. I had to go to her to schedule a meeting and when I looked up she was crying and looking straight into my eyes! She needed to talk and told me about the situation with her cousin who has just recently been hospitalized. A second later I heard myself ministering to her and telling her to lift her cousin up to God. I also printed out Tommy Tenney's daily devotional from yesterday and wrote a note to her. I've been praying for her and her cousin ever since.

That was the first time I have EVER discussed my spiritual life at work—and it certainly won't be the last! I feel like God has re-arranged my DNA, and it is the most incredible feeling! Thank you for leading our group and helping to teach me about the power of praise and worship.

As I started to outwardly exercise my faith, God began to teach me and draw closer to me as I drew closer to Him. Just as He promises in His Word, "Draw near to God and He will draw near to you" (James 4:8).

June 5, 2005

Lord, today I submitted to You with my tithe and fasting. I am seeking Your face and, on faith, decided today to obey Your Word and give my first true tithe to You. I want You; I need You; I long to see Your face, Lord. Cleanse me of all that is of this world. Purge from my being anything that is not of You. I am learning and growing at lightning speed. I pray for wisdom and discernment that the Holy Spirit will teach me what You want me to know. Lord, I know You have awesome plans for my life, and I completely submit to You. Guide me, lead me and use me. Father, I am learning to give, pray and fast as You direct me. I want all of You. Come to me—I must see Your face. Show me Your Glory, Lord!

On June 26, 2005, I made this journal entry following a trip Barb and I took in celebration of her birthday:

Thank You, Father God, for an awesome weekend! We went to Hershey, Pennsylvania, to see Beth Moore. Beth talked about Your wisdom and how Your wisdom is what we need to seek. We each wrote down the issues and things that we would seek Your wisdom for. We have been struggling with our relationship—our homosexuality and what Your Word says about it, what we hear from the preachers on TV, etc. We want to do Your will and only retain as part of our lives those things that are pleasing to You, removing all that would move us from the center of Your will. For weeks we have been discussing this and actually grieving over what might happen, over what we might hear from You and what that would mean for our situation—our lives together. We discussed this Friday night as well. We are prepared to separate if that is what You want us to do.

A lady from our women's group attended the event with us; we saved a seat for her Friday night because she had to work late. She was going to stay with us at the hotel but after the conclusion of Friday's session she decided to drive back home to come back with her friend on Saturday morning. We believe that You set that up so we could spend time talking Friday evening. On Saturday morning when we got to the Giant Center I could feel Your presence. I was very excited and felt that You would move powerfully in our lives. The conference was awesome! We studied Your Word in Proverbs about wisdom and I felt You spoke to us, telling us we were to remain together and to learn from each other about Your love.

We went to the amusement park and had a wonderful time! It brought out the kid in each of us. That evening we walked back to our car and had to go through hundreds of young people who were drinking in preparation for a rock concert. We could feel Satan's evil presence in the very parking lot where only hours earlier thousands of women had just come out of a time of powerful praise and worship of You! Lord, Your Spirit is alive within me and I can feel things of the spirit that I could never sense before. I love that You live inside me and guide me daily. I am so in love with You, Lord—I can't get enough of You and Your Word. This morning as we were driving back home discussing all we had experienced, our friend called and reconfirmed what we truly felt was Your word to us about staying together. She said she could feel the Holy Spirit working in us. Thank You, Father, for confirming to us what we felt You were saying. I pray that we will always remain open and receptive to hear Your voice. Please continue to teach me. I want to know You. I want to know what Your Word says. I want complete understanding and wisdom. God, teach me so I can better serve You on this earth. Praise and honor and glory to You, almighty Father. In Jesus' name I pray, amen!

As I was seeking God's will for my life, I continued to try out different things that I was learning about in my daily Bible study. I found myself becoming more generous and putting other's needs and desires above my own. One day Clarise had a problem with her car. It had to be put in the repair shop for several days, and she mentioned this in passing to me. I decided to loan her my car for as long as she needed it. This was the first time I ever considered loaning something of value to anyone. Following is an email that I sent to her upon getting my car back from her. She had cleaned it and had it professionally detailed before returning it to me:

July 11, 2005

Words cannot express the depth of my appreciation for what you are pouring into me spiritually by both your love and by your example!

The awesome gift of a beautifully detailed car was just the beginning of an incredible day yesterday. I've been praying for manifestation and increase of the fruit of the Spirit in my life "But the fruit of the Spirit is love, joy, peace, patience, kindness, goodness, faithfulness, gentleness and self-control" (Gal. 5:22-23 NIV) and I've also been fasting and praying for an increased awareness and sensitivity to hear the voice of God and to be obedient to His Word. Your graceful acceptance of my gift to you as well as the great care with which you treated the gift was a wonderful example to me because, like you, I also experience difficulty in asking for help and receiving gifts. "With this in mind, we constantly pray for you, that our God may count you worthy of his calling, and that by his power he may fulfill every good purpose of yours and every act prompted by your faith" (2 Thess. 1:11 NIV) speaks to both of us in the shared encounter. And to you who sows generously into the lives of every woman in our class, "Remember this: Whoever sows sparingly will also reap sparingly, and whoever sows generously will also reap generously" (2 Cor. 9:6 NIV).

I want to share with you what happened to me after the incredibly powerful praise and worship portion of the second service yesterday. I went upstairs to catch the end of Myrna's class where she was discussing the baptism of the Holy Spirit and the gift of speaking in tongues. I felt a very uncomfortable stirring in my soul that really made me nervous. When Myrna asked who wanted to receive the baptism of the Holy Spirit and the gift of speaking in tongues, I had to accept. I now have a powerful prayer language to draw me even closer to my greatest consuming passion: El Shaddai, the all-sufficient One; Adonai, LORD, Master; Jehovah-Jireh, the LORD will provide. I feel like I am moving at the speed of light toward the light of the world. I just can't get enough of HIM. I actually got upset this morning because I had to go to work—all I wanted to do is stay home and study all of the materials you introduced last night and all of the scriptures Myrna referenced regarding the Holy Spirit. I have been in the Bible all morning (before leaving the house on the train and secretly at my desk).

Because of your Sunday night class and because of getting to know, work and worship with you, my life has been altered forever! "For we are God's workmanship, created in Christ Jesus to do good works, which God prepared in advance for us to do" (Eph. 2:10 NIV).

"Be imitators of God, therefore, as dearly loved children and live a life of love, just as Christ loved us and gave himself up for us as a fragrant offering and sacrifice to God" (Eph. 5:1-2 NIV).

Following are entries in my journal.

July 13, 2005

Lord, Your Word is coming alive for me as I read and learn from the Bible! I am so excited about digging into Your Word and transforming my mind and my soul. Father, I feel the physical change You are inspiring in me: my mind is being transformed. You know the thoughts that are no longer with me; You are renewing my mind. Praise and honor and glory to You forever! Etch Your Word on my heart! "I have hidden your word in my heart that I might not sin against you" (Ps. 119:11 NIV*). Father, Your Word is absolute truth—I testify to this fact! I love You, Lord, with all my mind, heart and strength! "This is the covenant I will make with the house of Israel....I will put my laws in their minds and write them*

"I FEEL LIKE I AM MOVING AT THE SPEED OF LIGHT TOWARD THE LIGHT OF THE WORLD."

on their hearts. I will be their God, and they will be my people" (Heb. 8:10 NIV). "Love the LORD your God with all your heart and with all your soul and with all your strength" (Deut. 6:5 NIV). Thank You for Your Word! Thank You for revealing the meaning of Your Word and thank You for Your mercy and grace! Your humble servant, Deb

July 24, 2005

My God is an awesome God! Praise You, Lord, for You are worthy of all my praise! Today You did something awesome for me and I want to capture it in writing so I never forget this day! As You know, I've been studying Your Word and speaking to You daily as I build a relationship with You. I've been attending "The Women Who Worship God" Sunday evening class for several months now and each night we praise and worship You with song. I have wanted a tambourine to play in worship to You and have even gone to several music stores looking for just the right one and thought maybe I would find one in Israel. But this morning You surprised me with a miracle! On my way to volunteer at church this morning, I happened to see Your gift to me hanging on a post of a barbed wire fence of the cow field! You are such an awesome God! A white tambourine...perfect! I couldn't tell people fast enough what an awesome miracle I experienced! Thank You, God, for the gift! I will play it proudly for You in praise and worship! You are my Provider, Lord. Thank You!

This was the first instance I recall God specifically answering a prayer that was in my heart. He honored my desire to praise Him with the tambourine by performing a miracle for me. I wanted a tambourine of my own because many of the women in my women's group had their own praise instruments that they would bring to our Sunday night class for praise and worship. I was reminded of the Word of God, "If you abide in Me, and My words abide in you, you will ask what you desire, and it shall be done for you. By this My Father is glorified, that you bear much fruit; so you will be My disciples" (John 15:7-8). I had actually shopped around at several music stores around my home looking for the perfect tambourine, but I had not found the right one until God surprised me with my miracle.

CHAPTER 5

The Transition Years

(2000–2005)

Part II

If My people who are called by My name will humble themselves, and pray and seek My face, and turn from their wicked ways, then I will hear from heaven, and will forgive their sin and heal their land.

2 Chronicles 7:14

I spent the majority of the summer studying for the LSAT on my own and taking practice tests in preparation for the actual exam at the beginning of October. Shortly after completing the LSAT and working on applications for entry into law school, I took a trip to Israel from October 8-20, 2005, with a group of people from my church. There I experienced God in a most powerful and intimate way. This trip had a great impact on my growing faith. I got to see many of the places described in the Bible firsthand, which has really impacted my understanding of the Scriptures ever since. Following are a few of my journal entries recorded during that trip.

October 11, 2005

Lord, I love You with all my heart, soul and mind! I am so honored to walk in Your footsteps over 2000 years after You left this earth and ascended into heaven to Your throne on high! I love this land! Lord, continue to bless me with Your presence. I now have a shofar to bring You honor and praise along with my holy tambourine! Today was awesome—it started on the Mount of Beatitudes where our group was the first to arrive. We read Your Holy Scripture recorded in Matthew 5 as I looked over the Sea of Galilee. I was also baptized in the Jordan River today. Lord, what an awesome experience. Lord, I love You deeper today than any other day. Continue to teach me and show me Your ways, O Lord.

October 13, 2005

Lord, today is Yom Kippur, the Day of Atonement for Your chosen people. I pray today that You listen to their prayers, forgive their sins and show Yourself to them in a mighty way, Lord. Your Word tells us to love Your chosen people and to pray for their peace and the peace of Jerusalem. I stand with my Jewish brothers today, Lord, in reverence of You and also ask for the forgiveness of my sins. Lord, I seek Your will for my life. I am meeting people in this country who heard Your voice and obeyed Your command. Lord, I pray that I would have the strength and faith to be obedient to anything You would ask me to do, say or be. Lord, I feel Your mighty awesome power here on the shores of the Sea of Galilee...walking where You walked, and seeing the landscape that was so familiar to You as You walked on the face of this earth in a human body nearly 2000 years ago.

Thank You for Your revelation to me this morning about why You spelled out in such detail the laws and regulations and rituals the Jews were to follow in the book of Leviticus. These were the standard operating procedures that Your people were to follow when they were scattered to the four corners of the earth so they could and would remain a people—a holy chosen race even when they could not be together. It's just like the military unit that gets separated in battle and needs to function independently but as a single unit even when separated. Lord, I get so excited in my spirit when You reveal these things to me. I open the eyes and ears of my heart to You and wait expectantly for Your next revelation. I love You, Lord, with all my heart, strength, mind and soul.

"MAY I BE AN INSTRUMENT OF YOUR LOVE ON THIS EARTH."

October 17, 2005

Lord, I am learning so much about the history of Christianity and about our Jewish heritage, and I am beginning to understand our relationship over history and in the present day. I am so blessed to be here in Israel. Lord, You set this up for me as a step in my faith and a tool to teach me what You would have me know. I recognize Your fingerprint on this trip and my encounters with people, places and things in this land. Thank You, Lord, for eternal love and for thinking about and caring for me in a most intimate way. I pray You continue to educate me and lead me along Your path so I may do Your will and be an instrument of Your love on this earth.

October 20, 2005

Lord, it is just after midnight and I am sitting on the airplane headed home. This morning was cold and rainy; winter is coming to the Holy

City. Today we visited the House of Prayer for all Nations. From there we could see the Mount of Olives where You will be coming back as written in Zechariah 14:4: "And in that day His feet will stand on the Mount of Olives, which faces Jerusalem on the east...." Jayne sounded my shofar from that spot. She then blessed it and blessed me. What a powerful experience! The shofar has already called for You, Lord, from Mount Zion in the direction of the Mount of Olives. Lord, You have so much to teach me. I want to know You more every day and learn more about what You want me to know about history and the Bible. Lord, I pray for Your anointing on me to share what You would have me to share about what I learned here in the Holy Land with anyone You would have me reach and teach when I return home. You have blessed me beyond measure. Teach me to worship You with the shofar so that my playing of this instrument of praise to You will inspire others to seek You and stir their souls to worship You. Lord, I pray for the peace of Jerusalem. I pray for a deeper understanding of Your Word. I pray for wisdom and an ever-open heart to receive all You would have me receive, to Your glory.

Lord, I know You have a calling on my life and I want nothing more than to honor You. Lord, I pray that I will continue to seek You and feel Your presence as strongly as I have over this past week and a half. I want to be so much closer to You on a daily basis. Please, Lord, nudge my spirit throughout each day for the next month to turn to You and worship You. Holy Spirit, I depend on You to teach me and counsel me to worship God.

October 21, 2005

Adonai, praise and honor and glory to You forever! I join all of the heavenly hosts in worshipping You, God Most High, the Ancient of Days—hallelujah! Thank You, Lord, for Your anointing on me and my shofar! When I returned home yesterday and lifted the shofar to praise You from my house in West Virginia, the sweetest notes of praise came forth with ease. You are so awesome, Lord! The last note that came from that instrument was on Mount Zion! God, You are so good to me!

Continuing to Pursue the LSAT

When I returned from Israel, I received my test score for the LSAT that I had taken on October 1st and wrote the following journal entry:

October 23, 2005

Lord, as You know, I received my LSAT score via email yesterday and was extremely disappointed in my score...the score I received was lower than any practice test I took. Lord, I choose to praise You in the face of this disappointing news—Your will be done—lead me in what You would have me do. If law school is my own desire and not Yours, make it clear to me; I sit at Your feet and await Your direction for my life.

I spent some time over the next few days praying about and talking to others about the LSAT and my dreams of going to law school.

October 28, 2005

Lord, as I discovered in Israel, nothing happens by chance—Your hand is in everything we do if we would only open our eyes to see! I want to thank You for Your answer to my prayers concerning law school, whether I should retake the LSAT or trust that You will make a way for me if I surrender and trust You. Despite the Officer Assignment Board's recommendation to the Admiral that he not grant my assignment for Full-Time University Training because I have too many years of service already, he overruled them and signed off on my Full-time University Training request. Lord, You are so good and faithful!

I also got a powerful word from You yesterday morning regarding retaking the LSAT—I opened my lunchbox to see the answer: "Proverbs 3:7." I've been reading Proverbs 3:5-6 for months and overlooking Proverbs 3:7. "Trust in the LORD with all your heart and lean not on your own understanding; in all your ways acknowledge him, and he will make your paths straight. Do not be wise in your own eyes; fear the LORD and shun evil" (Prov. 3:5-7 NIV*). I believe You want me to trust You.*

"I WANT NOTHING MORE THAN TO SERVE YOU IN A WAY THAT PLEASES AND HONORS YOU."

The Women Who Worship God dance group that I was a part of continued to practice and perform at various venues. In fact, I was one of four soloists for the liturgical dance we performed to the song "Lord, You Are Holy." This was absolutely amazing, given the fact that I never believed I could dance, let alone perform as a soloist before people.

October 31, 2005

Lord, I completely trust You…continue to teach me to worship You with the shofar and with dance. I so enjoyed our praise dance to "Lord, You Are Holy" on Friday night. Lord, continue to strengthen my faith and begin to teach me how to share my faith, breaking down self-imposed barriers. Give me the wisdom and words to win souls for You, Lord. I want nothing more than to serve You in a way that pleases and honors You.

December 11, 2005

Lord, today is my 42nd birthday and I have much to be thankful for. I praise You and continue to walk in Your light—only going to the edge of the light and waiting for You to move forward so I can follow in Your footsteps. As You know, I received the disappointing news from Georgetown University on Thursday that I did not get accepted into their law program. You, Lord, know what is best for me and You see the beginning and the end. Lord, You have a plan for my life and I know that Your plans are greater than mine for my life. I will retest for the LSAT on February 4th at USC in California and will apply to the other schools in D.C. I don't believe that You would open the doors for me to be accepted into the Full-Time University Training in NOAA and then not get accepted into any of the schools I apply to. Lord, I love You with all my heart, mind and soul. I will walk in Your ways for eternity. Love always, Your servant Deb

"Coming Out"

On this same day, I approached Clarise and told her that Barb and I wanted to "come clean" with the women in our ministry (believing that nobody in the group knew we were gay). She suggested that we meet with the pastor to discuss this before talking to the women's group, so we scheduled a meeting.

December 18, 2005

Lord, You are so awesome! You have been revealing Yourself to me all week and I praise and thank You for that. You are revealing past areas of sin in my life and showing how You have delivered me from all of that darkness and brought me into the light where You strengthen and mold me and refine me day by day. You don't move too fast for me—You walk with me every step of the way and put people in my path to minister to me. Thank You for the growth, encouragement and revelation that You are bringing Barb and I by way of Your Word. Lord, Your Word is nourishment for my soul—I must have Your Word every day. Thank You for feeding me and teaching me. Lord, I can hardly bear the thought of what You have done for me: while still a sinner You protected and kept me for this day. I am growing so much in love with You and can't go very long in the day without thinking of You. I am so grateful for the people You have placed in my path. Lord, I love Clarise and all of the women in our Sunday night worship and praise group. Thank You for putting all of us together to grow in Your love. Thank You for bringing Pastor Scott to our church to minister to us and heal our broken church. Lord, Barb and I spoke with Clarise last Sunday about our relationship and our desire to become members of Covenant and she is joining us this coming Wednesday evening at 5 p.m. to discuss our relationship with each other and the church. Lord, I pray that You minister to us through Scott and Clarise and that we can hear with Your ears and see with Your eyes to receive the message that You have for us. I love You, Lord, with my whole heart, mind and soul! Yours truly, Deb

December 21, 2005

Praise You, Jesus! Thank You for the meeting with Clarise and Scott this evening. Barb and I were given a chance to talk about our relationship with each other and with this church in a totally loving and non-confrontational manner. Lord, You were there in the midst of us as the four of us spoke, listened and tried to understand each other. We exposed our souls and were completely honest with them about where we are now in our walk with You, Lord, and where we have come from in the past. I know You have a plan and purpose for our lives and, Lord, I know You are refining me in the fire day by day. Use us to further Your kingdom, show us and teach us Your ways, O Lord.

I lay at Your feet in total submission; make me an instrument of Your peace. Show me how to live a holy life; show me the areas of sin in my life; by Your Word continue to reveal to me what needs to change in order for me to be pleasing to You. Turn Your face toward me, O Lord; let me gaze into Your eyes. I love You, Jesus, with all my heart, mind, soul and strength. I want to please You. I want You to draw near to me. Let me be an example of love and holiness after You finish refining me. Let me not be a stumbling block for anyone seeking to live a holy life. Your praises are continually on my tongue—I love You, Lord! Thank You for the godly people You have placed in my path, Lord; they are precious to me. I feel honored to have been given the time and loving attention that we received tonight. Thank You, Lord. Continue to bless and strengthen Your servants. I am Yours, Lord; make me in Your image by continuing to refine me. I am submitting to Your will for my life. Your humble servant and loving daughter, Debora

During this first meeting, I remember Pastor Scott asking me why I labeled myself as homosexual. I answered that I was born that way and felt I needed to tell him who I was because my lifestyle didn't conform to what the church teaches. He said he saw me as a child of God and that I needed no other label. I began to think about what he said.

December 22, 2005

Thank You, Lord Jesus, for the revelation this morning! I now see why my path back to You has been exactly set. My lesbian partner in Florida brought me back to You in the early 90s as I began to attend Metropolitan Community Church. I was there all those years as I started seeking You also to be exposed to distorted truth and twisted interpretation of the Scriptures. Then upon moving to D.C., You introduced me to Barb because we were destined for Your work. I started and stopped my interest in volunteering at the church because that was in Your plans for me, while Barb started and stopped interest in Clarise's "Power of a Praying Woman" class. The reason for the rocky starts—Satan hates the fact that we are drawing closer to You! I love You, Lord, and want to stay in the center of this path that You have me on. Continue to light that path and nudge us along because I am excited about where You are leading us!

GOD HAD BEEN WORKING BEHIND THE SCENES MY ENTIRE LIFE.

I began to recognize how God had been working behind the scenes my entire life and how Satan had tried to abort God's plans for me. When I listened to the voice of the enemy of my soul, I was on the path to death and destruction. "There is a way that seems right to a man, but its end is the way of death" (Prov. 14:12; 16:25).

December 24, 2005

Good morning, Jesus! Thank You for the continued revelation and, again, thank You for the godly people who care about us. I have been reading a book that Pastor Scott loaned to me, A Strong Delusion: Confronting the "Gay Christian" Movement *by Joe Dallas. The Holy Spirit has convicted me that my homosexuality is sin. I repent and ask for Your forgiveness and deliverance.*

Lord, Barb and I are moving furniture today and setting up two bedrooms in our home. We pray for Your strength in helping us through this traumatic period. Yesterday we removed our rings and I researched how we can dissolve our legal civil union that we entered into on April 22, 2001. I don't see a solution there because what I found out is that Vermont law requires one or both parties to a civil union to be a resident of Vermont for six months before the family law court will consider dissolution of a civil union. Lord, I pray that You provide a way for us to dissolve this legal union; nothing is impossible for You, and this thing I place at Your feet. I will not fret over it and will await Your guidance. I pray that as we reveal the change in our relationship to family and friends that Your words and Spirit take over to allow the listeners to receive the message in a way pleasing to You. We want to do Your will and help others understand that we were wrong—we were out of Your will for our lives—and we want to help our gay friends realize what has been revealed to us. Lord, keep us and protect us as we work through this transition. I love You with all my heart, mind, soul and strength! Debora

The Holy Spirit, without a doubt, revealed to me and to Barb that we had been living outside of the will of God for our lives during our scripture reading and prayer time together. Finally, I recognized that homosexuality is wrong and that God does not condone homosexuality. There was no specific scripture that I recall reading on that day; rather, it was more of an answer to the prayer that I kept praying—I kept asking God to reveal His truth to me. Barb asked me if I still thought I was born gay, and I said no. I experienced a peaceful "knowing" in my spirit that God's answer to my prayer was that He did not create me gay, that I had been living outside of His will. Once we fully understood this and got the message from God and not man, we both decided to act immediately. We acted decisively and changed our living arrangements inside our home.

To solidify my commitment to Jesus Christ, I also decided that I would have the ring that once symbolized my "marriage" to Barb, transformed into a wedding band symbolizing my new commitment to the Lord. I contacted the artist who designed the rings that Barb and I had purchased for our civil union and asked if he would modify my ring to accommodate a custom design. He added a cross to the face of the ring with the symbols for alpha and omega (the beginning and end) on either side of the cross and a sunrise burst behind the cross. I also had one of my favorite scripture references inscribed on the inside of the ring: Proverbs 9:10, which says, "The fear of the LORD is the beginning of wisdom, and the knowledge of the Holy One is understanding." Every day when I look at my ring, I remember what Jesus did for me and am reminded of my commitment to Him.

December 24, 2005 p.m.

Lord, this evening is Christmas Eve. Barb and I spent the whole day moving and disassembling the spare bedroom and office to set up Barb's room on the other side of the house. Tonight we are sleeping in different rooms for the first night. It is extremely hard for me because sleeping next to Barb is one of the most comforting things for me. I love feeling her next to me and knowing she is there when I wake up in the night—listening for her breathing. I know we are only on opposite sides of this small house and still love each other deeply, but this feels like a separation—a death—and it hurts! Lord, I pray that You comfort me and help me through this.... Lord, You are my rock and my salvation; I love You with all my heart and will continue to walk in Your path as You purify and refine me. Strengthen me and comfort me; You are my salvation! Love, Debora

December 25, 2005

Jesus, as You so often do, You continually reveal Yourself to me. In our morning readings in Hebrews, the following verses hit hard after my first night alone in my bed with Barb sleeping on the other side of the house. "If we deliberately keep on sinning after we have received the knowledge of the truth, no sacrifice for sins in left, but only a fearful expectation of judgment and of raging fire that will consume the enemies of God" (Heb. 10:26-27 NIV).

Now that we know without a doubt that homosexuality is sin—it was revealed to us and is now "knowledge of the truth"—we have to turn our lives around. Again in Hebrews it says, "Endure hardship as discipline; God is treating you as sons. For what son is not disciplined by his father?" (Heb. 12:7 NIV). And, "Our fathers disciplined us for a little while as they thought best; but God disciplines us for our good, that we may share in his holiness. No discipline seems pleasant at the time, but painful. Later on, however, it produces a harvest of righteousness and peace for those who have been trained by it" (Heb. 12:10-11 NIV).

Obedience—No Matter What

Once I realized conclusively that homosexuality was wrong in God's eyes and that He did not want me living my life as a lesbian, I made up in my mind that I would turn my back on the life I had lived for so long and begin walking in the truth of God's Word no matter how hard it would turn out to be. Barb and I made a commitment to God and to each other that we would do whatever He required of us.

December 26, 2005

Lord, I am still struggling with all of this. I am reading the books Scott gave us to read and feel different emotions. I am embarrassed that I believed that my lifestyle was within Your will for my life and also am angry about the deception preached at MCC that I believed! I am deeply sorry for living my life so far outside Your will and ask Your forgiveness. You know all of the sin in my life—things I did, thought and believed that I can't even write down—cleanse me with Your blood; forgive my sins and empower the Holy Spirit within me to continue to reveal areas of sin in my life so I can change anything that is not pleasing to You. I love You, Lord, with all my heart, mind, soul and strength. Love, Debora

I went through a period of experiencing shame, humiliation and godly sorrow. Again, I saw my own life experience in Scripture: "Surely, after my turning, I repented; and after I was instructed, I struck myself on the thigh; I was ashamed, yes, even humiliated, because I bore the reproach of my youth" (Jer. 31:19). "For godly sorrow produces repentance leading to salvation, not to be regretted; but the sorrow of the world produces death" (2 Cor. 7:10).

December 26, 2005 p.m.

Lord, Barb and I had a conversation just before going to bed because both of us are feeling like we are going through a grieving process. We both shared about our feelings and insecurities and I believe You made it clear to us that the only change we are making here is that we are sleeping in separate rooms so that our one bedroom doesn't become a stumbling block for anyone who is looking at our lives. Others don't have the benefit of knowing that You began to reveal Your will to us a year ago regarding sexual relations and that we have abstained ever since. Continue to reveal Yourself to us and help us to redefine in our own minds our relationship so we can communicate that to friends and family in an honest, non-threatening way. All we want is to do Your will and have Your power and glory manifested in our lives. Lord, I ask You to fill me with the Holy Spirit. Manifest all of the gifts of Your Spirit in my life—You are my rock, my fortress, my salvation, my counselor, healer, teacher and God. I want all You have for me! Love always, Debora

"I am deeply sorry for living my life so far outside Your will...."

December 27, 2005 a.m.

Lord, in Your Word this morning in Revelation You say, "Those whom I love I rebuke and discipline. So be earnest, and repent. Here I am! I stand at the door and knock. If anyone hears my voice and opens the door, I will come in and eat with him, and he with me. To him who overcomes, I will give the right to sit with me on my throne, just as I overcame and sat down with my Father on his throne" (Rev. 3:19-21 NIV). Thank You for Your Word! Thank You for Your impeccable timing—we repent of our sins and invite You in to eat with us. Lord, I love You. Thank You for loving me and rebuking and disciplining me. Please reveal to me any other areas of sin in my life so I can sit with You on Your throne in heaven. Your daughter, Debora

December 27, 2005 p.m.

Lord, I was praying on the way to the train station this morning and afterward heard something on the Christian radio station that was a revelation to me. The preacher was talking about how the serpent tricked Eve in the Garden of Eden, deceiving her by twisting the meaning of Your Word with respect to eating of the forbidden fruit. I equate this to the way MCC twisted the truth regarding Your Word as it relates to homosexuality. Keep revealing Yourself to me and teach me what You would have me to know.

As I continued to pray that God would reveal areas of my life that needed to change, He honored those prayers and revealed things to me regarding other areas of my life. Now, when I teach others about God and prayer, I refer to this prayer as a "dangerous prayer." If you are not willing to allow God to change things in your life that need changing, don't pray for Him to reveal those things to you. God answers your prayers when you pray in accordance with His will.

December 28, 2005

Lord, You continue to amaze me. A couple of weeks ago You brought to my mind that I need to get "right" with my legal records. I have been claiming Florida as my state of residence and didn't change it when I moved here. I inquired about this a couple of years ago and was told I could continue to claim Florida and not have to pay state income tax. I filled out the paperwork to be effective on January 1, 2006, to claim West Virginia and begin paying state taxes. Lord, I am being obedient to Your will and direction in my life and You continue to amaze me.

In case you think that making major changes in your life to align your life with the will of God is easy, I have decided to be real in this book and share all of the ups and downs in my emotions and experiences throughout this transition in my life. Sometimes it seems I am on the top of the mountain one day, and within a day or two, I am crashing in the valley below. That is exactly how I was experiencing life day by day during this transition.

December 30, 2005

Lord, I need You! I am so lonely. I don't know who I am anymore. Everything I know about who I am is now turned upside down. I'm confused, angry, hurt and lonely. I am struggling with all of these changes and disconnections. Help me! In addition to all of this emotional turmoil, I can't focus to study for the LSAT I need to take on February 4th. I need You! I need a miracle! Tell me what You want me to do!

December 31, 2005

Lord, I look back over the past year and You have been faithful as always. I read what I wrote on January 1 of this year about wanting to dance—You made it possible for me in a big way! Now I dance for You, for Your glory, and will continue to dance in praise to You in the coming year. You have worked mightily in my life this past year…I want to strengthen and deepen my relationship with women of God. I want to continue to grow closer and more intimate with You, Lord. I seek Your face. Please continue to refine me, teach me, mold me into the person You want me to be for Your kingdom. Fill me with the Holy Spirit to overflowing. Teach me to worship You with the shofar and dance. All praise and honor and glory to You, Almighty Father—Ancient of Days, Abba Father forever and ever! Love, Debora

CHAPTER 6

The New Beginning Years

(2006–2008)

Part I—2006

Therefore, if anyone is in Christ, [s]he is a new creation; old things have passed away; behold, all things have become new.

2 CORINTHIANS 5:17

The year 2006 was truly a year of new beginnings for me. This was the year when my life took a 180-degree change in direction from the way I had been living most of the previous year. This was the year I really began to grow in my Christian faith as I struggled with the changes I was experiencing in my life.

January 1, 2006 a.m.

Lord, today is a day of new beginnings, the beginning of a new year. I give You the firstfruits of myself this day. I pray for wisdom and a fresh infusion of the Holy Spirit. Teach me to worship You with power and submission. I want to spend time with You behind the curtain in the Holy of Holies—I want to bathe myself in Your glory so Your radiance will go out from me and touch a troubled and lonely world. Bathe me in Your glory so I exude joy. Teach me to live the joyful life You want me to live. Make me complete in You, O Lord. Teach me to be a worshipper; strengthen me each day with Your wisdom and power. Lord, use me in a mighty way this year. Keep me on the middle of the path toward righteousness as You refine me; reveal areas of my being that need change in order to be in line with Your will. Cleanse me with the blood of the Lamb, my Lord and Savior, Jesus Christ. Amen!

January 1, 2006 p.m.

Lord Jesus, what a most powerful and awesome day! I went to church early today and spent some time talking to Clarise about the struggles and pain I have been experiencing this past week. I also told her of the wonderful ways You have showed Yourself mighty as well. One reading that she did for our unity service was from Hebrews—"a call to persevere" that spoke to me in such a powerful way, especially after I wrote to You this morning before leaving for church. "Therefore, brothers, since we have confidence to enter the Most Holy Place by the blood of Jesus, by a new and living way opened for us through the curtain, that is, his body, and since we have a great priest over the house of God, let us draw near to God with a sincere heart in full assurance of faith, having our hearts sprinkled to cleanse us from a guilty conscience and having our bodies washed with pure water. Let us hold unswervingly to the hope we profess, for he who promised is faithful. And let us consider how we may spur one another on toward love and good deeds. Let us not give up meeting together, as some are in the habit of doing, but let us encourage one another—and all the more as you see the Day approaching" (Heb. 10:19-25 NIV).

Lord, You made a way for us today to have Pastor Scott and the elders (Al, Harry & Charlie) come to our house after the service, along with their wives and our dear friends Clarise, Jayne, and Renee, to bless our home and bless us on the first day of the new year 2006. We were so honored that they love us so much to come here and take time away from their families to witness our miracle and share in our joy for the revelation You gave us and our walk with You! Tonight we were able to continue in our miracle when we shared with our women's group what You have been doing in our lives. Lord, I have never felt the depth of love that I experienced today and I know without a doubt that it was all for Your glory! Praise You, Lord—You are my greatest desire, my deepest love. Continue to use me and teach me Your will for my life. I worship You and give my life over to You. Praise You, El Shaddai! Love, Debora

One thing about this day that I will never forget is the true unconditional love shown to me by Jayne. She was standing with me and was crying. She looked me in the eyes and said she could see and feel my pain. She said she could see that I loved Barb and that I was doing what I was doing to align my life with the Word of God.

The next several months proved to be a painful transition for Barb and me out of the homosexual life, but we were determined to do what was right. We were determined to follow Jesus at all costs. We were determined to live out what the Bible says in Luke 9:23: "Then He [Jesus] said to them all, 'If anyone desires to come after Me, let him deny himself, and take up his cross daily, and follow Me.'"

For me, it felt like a physical death, the loss of physical touch and the struggle to redefine myself. I didn't know who I was anymore, because I had identified myself as a lesbian for eighteen years and had actually fully convinced myself that I had always been gay. I fully believed that I was born gay and that was why I was never able to connect sexually with my boyfriend so many years ago.

Barb and I also lost our place in the gay community, which had become our surrogate family structure. We were no longer accepted in the gay community—we had betrayed them by denouncing our homosexuality—and yet we did not feel as though we fit into the heterosexual world either. I thank God for the healthy heterosexual men and women who surrounded me with love as I suffered through this transition. I don't know if I would have made it without their support of love and prayers.

As I drew closer to Jesus, He began to reveal to me the things that had occurred in my past that led me to embrace that life and God began to heal those deep wounds. I began to learn about the root causes of homosexuality. For me, some of these root causes were a broken relationship with my mother as a teen, my overly sensitive temperament, sexual abuse by men and socialization into homosexuality by my first lesbian partner. I also grieved the loss of what my life could have been if I had married and had children, realizing then at the age of forty-two that I might never marry and have a family of my own.

February 13, 2006

I praise You, Lord! I read an article today in Charisma magazine entitled "How to help self-destructive teens." It is about self-mutilation by cutting or pulling hair. It really struck a deep chord in me, remembering the years of self-destructive hair pulling I experienced in my own life. Lord, You have been working so powerfully in my life—driving out my fears, insecurities, sin and rebellion little by little and all the while strengthening me until I have increased enough to take possession of the land You have for me, a land flowing with milk and honey! I love You so much! Continue to do Your good work in me; continue to speak to me and lead me in Your ways, O Lord. Continue to speak through me into this dark and hurting world. Continue to strengthen the bonds of love and friendship between my church family and me. Continue to heal me and sanctify me, Lord!

February 14, 2006, email to Clarise

God is so awesome! He never ceases to amaze me!

I am so amazed at the work that Christ is doing in my life, for me personally and through my willingness to set aside self and let Him work through me. I want to share with you a revelation that the Lord gave me last night in our daily scripture readings from Exodus.

"But I will not drive them out in a single year, because the land would become desolate and the wild animals too numerous for you. Little by little I will drive them out before you, until you have increased enough to take possession of the land" (Exod. 23:29-30 NIV).

"I AM SO AMAZED AT THE WORK THAT CHRIST IS DOING IN MY LIFE."

The message to me was this: When I surrender my will to the Lord and allow Him to make me a new creation in Him, He drives out the evil (sin, self-doubt, insecurity, pride, whatever is not pleasing in His sight) little by little—all the while strengthening me and increasing my confidence in trusting Him so I can take possession of the new land that He has promised me.

Thank you for supporting and encouraging me as I take each new step in faith!

February 24, 2006

Okay, Lord, it is entirely up to You. I received my LSAT score this afternoon and it was 149. Still much lower than the scores generally accepted for all law schools around here. I need a miracle now! You put this desire in my heart and paved the way for NOAA to finance my education; now You have to compel a school to accept me. I leave it in Your hands.

March 3, 2006

Lord, I love You so much! I can't describe in words how magnificent You are and how deeply I love You! Today was an incredible day! This morning I sent an email to Pastor Scott and asked him if he would baptize Barb and me at the unity service on March 26th—his last day with us at Covenant. He agreed to do it and we are so excited.

Lord, we want to rededicate our lives to You and publicly proclaim our faith and trust in You as we die to our previous sinful past and are reborn into Your light and life. Jesus, I want nothing more than to be in Your presence at all times; Your Word is life and You sustain me. Without You I do not exist. We just paid off the cars and credit card after writing a large freewill offering check; You have honored Your Word and blessed us beyond belief. Jesus, You are my rock, my Savior, my Prince of Peace, my Comforter and my salvation. Thank You for loving me and reaching out to me when I was so far away. Thank You for protecting and watching over me all the years I turned from You and denied You even existed. Love always, Debora

Healing from Homosexuality

March 5, 2006

"Let My Life Song Sing to You"—that's the title of a new song that sums up how I want my life to honor You. This evening I shared a portion of my story with our women's group. What a powerful exercise and what a powerful experience as we get to know each other and go

beneath the outer surface that we show to the world to expose those inner parts of our being to other people. We help each other heal as You heal us individually. Lord, You are so awesome as You work through us and in us. Thank You for the safe environment and relationships we are building. Thank You for healing me and allowing me to lower my barriers and let others in. Thank You for the friendships and relationships where I can learn to love and be loved as You so freely pour out Your love on me, blessing me every day. I worship You, Lord! I glorify and magnify Your holy name! Teach me and continue to refine me as You mold me into who I am for You. Continue to strengthen me to step out in boldness and speak to others about Your mighty love and works in my life. As I look back at my trials and tribulations, I see that You always had someone there to listen to me and care about me and I would like to do that for others. I am in awe of Your love for me!

March 8, 2006

Lord, You have been revealing to me the power of Your Word today in various ways. The first was in our reading in Deuteronomy: "They are not just idle words for you—they are your life" (Deut. 32:47a NIV). Later I heard on the radio that Your Word was not written to make us good people by following it; rather, the Word is for us to follow by faith and obedience to You. Obedience is what we should strive for. Your ways are not our ways.

This evening I saw Beth Moore on television and she was talking about the power of Your Word in Ephesians, which says we are to "take the helmet of salvation and the sword of the Spirit, which is the word of God" (Eph. 6:17 NIV). She emphasized that all of the other "armor of God" is used for defense but the sword is an offensive weapon. I need to learn and memorize Your Word to use as a weapon against the devil's schemes. Lord, teach me Your Word—write it with Your finger on my heart. Open my mind and eyes to know Your Word and have it infused into my inmost being so I will always walk in Your ways and know that I know that I know that I am in the center of Your will for my life! You are my God! I love You with my whole heart, mind and soul! Thank You, Lord, for loving me and watching over me.

March 10, 2006

Lord, as You know, this evening I received a rejection letter from American University Law School. I was disappointed and fear and doubt gripped me. Lord, I trust You to make a way for me because I believe this is what You have planned for my life. I lift my eyes up to You and place my trust in You! I love You, Lord, with all my heart, mind and soul.

March 11, 2006

Lord, I love You so much! You are amazing me once again as I read this new book of healing for my turn from homosexuality. For the second day in a row You lined up my scripture readings with what I am reading in this book about the prophetess Anna written about in Luke 2 who was in the temple courts when You were brought there by Your human parents to be circumcised on the eighth day.

Lord, thank You for blessing me and not destroying me for all of the years I turned my back on You and willfully sinned against You. Thank You for loving me and gently teaching me that homosexuality was wrong. Thank You for numbing my sexual desire as You heal my mind. I ask You to continue to renew my mind and infuse me with Your Word through the Holy Spirit who lives in me. Thank You, Lord!

March 13, 2006

Lord, I received another law school rejection letter today—this one from the University of Maryland. That is not the school You have for me. I'll wait for the right one. This morning on the train I began working on my personal mission statement to yesterday's servant community leader training at church. Part of the exercise had me looking back at the time line of my life and looking for patterns so I can recognize the warning signs in the future if they occur again. What I discovered is that those times that I allowed the love or lack of love from another human being to control my feelings of self-worth—if that love was violated—it sent me into a tailspin. I need to seek all of my love and self-worth from You, Lord—the perfect lover of my soul who will never leave me nor forsake me. You are Love and the only one I can trust unconditionally. Who I am in Your eyes is all that matters and I let my life song sing to You, Lord. May my very existence be pleasing to You, Lord.

March 19, 2006

Lord, last night we danced to "Lord, You Are Holy" at Wright Denny School in Charles Town at a fundraiser gospel concert and it was so powerful! Praising You in that way strengthens my soul in a way that nothing else does! I love You so much!

This morning, after the first service, Barb and I attended the Covenant New Members class. We are finally becoming members of this church. Lord, that is where it all began with Barb and I attending this class several years ago in 2003. Our brothers and sisters in Christ have loved us until You spoke into our lives, uncovered the sin in our lives and washed us clean. I thank You for the people of this church who did not turn their backs on us knowing that we were living a life outside Your will, but who continued to love us until You did the work in our lives. Lord, I will never be the same!

March 26, 2006—BAPTISM DAY!

Lord, You are so good! Today was our unity service at Covenant and Pastor Scott Hesler's last Sunday with us. Barb and I were baptized and it was such a powerful experience for me—I have been smiling all day! I spoke of my recommitment to You and that I was being re-baptized as an outward sign to my entire church family of my death to my sinful past and resurrection into the new abundant life that God has for me. I said that Paul tells us in Second Corinthians that if we are in Christ we are "a new creation; the old has gone, the new has come!" (2 Cor. 5:17 NIV). I told of my journey over the past year and how You, Lord, have completely transformed my life with the support of my spiritual family. I am growing in my love for You. I love You with all my heart, mind and soul. We also received our membership to Covenant this past week—Hallelujah—what an awesome work You have done in our lives. Lord, You are the Lord of my life. I hand over control of my entire being to You; mold me and use me to further Your kingdom. I am Yours, Lord!

"The Lord has completely transformed my life with the support of my spiritual family."

March 30, 2006

Lord, I thank You for placing wonderful people in my life to guide me on my spiritual journey. I went to the prayer meeting last night at church where I am learning more about how to pray. I have such powerful role models and mentors in Jayne, Sophia, Myrna and others. Scott and Clarise came to our house for dinner and fellowship this evening. We wanted to honor Scott for his role in our transformation before he leaves for his new church. He asked if we would be willing to come to his new church and speak about the miracles You have performed in our lives. This morning You told me that I need to work on a pamphlet to be distributed to churches about how to deal with people and their sin in a loving way that helps to bring them into the family and not drive them away. Lord, I ask for Your wisdom and discernment and Your will as I begin to think about this. You have a powerful ministry for me and I want to serve You with my life. I love You, Lord!

April 17, 2006

Lord, today I received the eighth rejection letter—this one from Dickinson School of Law. The last school I have applied to but have not yet heard from is University of the District of Columbia. I thank You for narrowing it down to the one school You have prepared for me in advance. That is the school I will go to this fall. I am believing You for this.

Strengthen my faith as I continue to walk in Your Word and trust in You. Lord, I pray that beginning right now You become for me my everything—my lover, my security, my counselor. Teach me to trust and hope in You alone, to not put other people or myself ahead of my love and relationship with You. You are the only one who never changes; Your Word never changes and always accomplishes what You set it out to accomplish. I desire to hide Your Word and Your truths in my heart—in my inmost being—so I can draw on Your Word and Your living water at any time. Teach me Your ways, O Lord. Teach me to love You alone. Teach me to trust You completely. I know You are refining me and making me more like You; please continue to work with me and to love me. Magnify Yourself in my life so I see only You, hear only You, taste only You, feel only You, smell only You. Heal me, O Lord; heal my areas of hurt and pain. Teach me to love You with complete and all-encompassing love. You are all I desire; You are all I need, Lord!

April 19, 2006

Lord, thank You for this day! Thank You for orchestrating my life. Today I shared with Mary what Barb and I have been going through with Your revelation to us of our sin, our repentance and Your mercy and grace. Help me to share the miracle with the rest of my family and friends as Your Spirit leads me to share. Lord, You are doing a great work in me and I ask You to equip me for Your ministry. Heal me where I need healing, cleanse me where I need cleansing, burn away the impurities where You find them in me. Search my heart and teach me Your ways.

Please continue to teach me to praise You with the shofar. Place Your anointing on my lips and fill me with Your spirit of praise in dance and the blowing of the shofar. Anoint my body to praise You—take away all of the shackles that have ever bound me in my ability to praise and worship You! You are my first love—stoke the flame of burning desire in my heart for You alone. Satisfy my every need. Let me feel Your presence, hear Your still small voice, feel Your breath upon me, hear Your heartbeat. Lord, I need You like I have never needed anything or anybody in my life before. I want to please You. I want to do Your will. I want to know You as You know me. I want to love You as much as You love me. Refine me, Lord!

April 20, 2006, email to Clarise and Pastor Scott

I had an incredible experience on the way to work this morning that I want to share with you while it is fresh in my mind. I was commuting on the train to Silver Spring and listening to my mp3 player—praise and worship music drowning out all other sounds around me, eyes closed—praying and pressing in closer to the Lord when it felt like a cargo strap let loose from my inner soul.

I really understood deep in my soul for the first time the MAGNITUDE of the miracle that God has performed in my life! I knew with a "head knowledge" that a miracle has occurred and have heard many other people say that a miracle has occurred—and have even said it myself—but riding the wave of emotion for the past several months as I have, it didn't resonate deep in my soul enough to break that bondage until today!

I was trapped in a life of sin and despair that was dragging me down to the depths of the grave for over twenty years, and at the time, I didn't even know it! I thought I was making my own way in this world and everything in my world was fine! All the while I was searching for love and acceptance and a sense of belonging from those who could never give me what my soul was desperate for, and at the same time I turned my back (and publicly denounced) the ONLY ONE who truly LOVES ME, has ALWAYS LOVED ME, will ALWAYS LOVE ME and is the ONLY SOURCE for what I have been searching for all of those years!

All the while GOD (who knew me from the beginning of time, created me in His hands, and breathed life into me)— that same God— watched over me for all of these years with tears in His eyes, protected me from harm, grieved when I hurt Him and sacrificed His only Son who was without sin to cover my abominable sin to save my wretched soul that should have been destroyed years ago for all of the evil I have committed in my lifetime! I didn't even deserve to be considered by Him, yet He loves me so much that He did consider me. He gently revealed to me the areas of sin in my life and placed people and circumstances in my path to lead me back to His loving embrace!

I THANK GOD that He protected me all these years (even when I tried to destroy myself) and allowed me to wake up each day on this earth until I turned back to Him, repented of my sin and invited Him to fully control my life FOR ETERNITY—or right now I would be burning in hell forever. I shudder to think that for one second He could have turned HIS back on ME and allowed me to be destroyed!

I want to shout from the mountaintops into the heavens: Hallelujah, Jesus! Thank You for loving me! Thank You for saving me! I will praise Your name forever! Hallelujah!

Going to Law School!

May 14, 2006, email to a large group of my friends who had been praying for me to get into law school

PRAISE THE LORD! God is truly awesome! He is true to His Word and His unfailing love!

I wanted to give you an update on where I stand on getting into law school. The Lord placed in me a desire to go to law school a couple of years ago, and ever since I have been working toward that goal. I have been given an incredible opportunity to attend law school free of charge through my job, while being paid my full salary—and I have an opportunity to go to school full-time for three years.

I took the required Law School Aptitude Test on October 1, 2005, but didn't score very well. I then took the test again on February 4th in an attempt to raise my score into a more acceptable range for the schools I was applying for. About three weeks later I received the disappointing

news that my score was still lower than what I believed I needed for acceptance to law school.

Still believing that God would make a way for me, I went ahead and applied to nine law schools within a 100-mile radius of my house. Over these past few months I have been receiving letters from these schools with the familiar, "We regret to inform you…" statement. In fact, eight of the nine schools sent me these letters. Then I received nothing for six weeks, every day checking the mailbox for that last letter that I was holding out hope for. Over the past six weeks I have been questioned by my employer numerous times: "Have you heard yet?" As fear and doubt would try to creep in, I would hold on to God's Word and faith in the one who put this desire in my heart and made a way for me where it seemed impossible. (The whole story surrounding my acceptance into the "full-time university training" program is another testimony in itself since that program was discontinued about three to four years ago and didn't even exist when I applied and was accepted—despite adamant opposition by a senior officer on the assignment board.)

Well, yesterday I received the letter from the last school: the University of the District of Columbia David A. Clarke School of Law. It had the familiar shape and weight. I opened it and was ecstatic to read, "The Admission Committee has reviewed your application and placed it on our waiting list." HALLELUJAH, JESUS! This is definitely NOT a rejection letter! My Lord and Savior has been working behind the scenes all this time making a way for me!

He is true to His Word.

May 27, 2006

Lord, I pray that You continue to reveal Yourself to me and continue to transform me into Your image. Lord, You revealed to me yesterday during our time together that You truly are transforming my life—from inside out. Lord, You know the terrible sin that was inside me, taking over my mind from time to time. I thank You, Jesus, for removing that completely by the shedding of Your blood on Calvary and from You seeking me and drawing me to You with Your unfailing love. Infuse me with that love—rush into me and fill me to overflowing with Your power. Flood me with Your Holy Spirit; burn away all impurities from my soul and mind and body and make me holy as You are holy. Lord. I have learned from the experiences You have exposed me to, what I need to know to get closer to You. You taught me through my service as Admiral's aide to learn the speech patterns, thought patterns and mannerisms of the one I serve in order to be an effective speechwriter. Lord, let me know You that well so I can be Your speechwriter. Be my mentor, Jesus! You taught me that through friendships, if I want a relationship with someone, I have to work at it. Lord, I want a relationship with You. I want You to call me friend. I want to be there for You as You are there for me. God, You taught me how much I broke Your heart when I turned from You and denied You. I have felt the pain of that heartbreak in the ending of my relationship with my first true love. The utter despair I experienced at rejection from my first love—Lord, I am so sorry I hurt You and turned away from You for so many years. Years You still longed for me and watched over me, hovering all around and over me as I grieved You. Lord, I will never leave You; You are my heart's desire! Lord, You taught me in revelation while reading Joshua 11 that in order to take possession of the promises You have for me, I have to totally destroy the enemy and claim what is mine. I have to completely destroy any shadow of doubt or fear that may rise up and try to keep me from Your promises. Jesus, You are all I want—all I need—be my everything…my lover, my security, my mentor, my coach, my best friend, my Lord and my God!

June 4, 2006

Jesus, You revealed to me this morning an area of pain in my life that has not yet been healed. During the church service the preacher stood in the place of all men who have hurt women emotionally, physically and sexually and asked for forgiveness. Lord, I broke down and was crying. You revealed to me that I still have unhealed areas of pain from my past. Lord, heal my wounds; You are the only one who can heal me. I ask You to give me the strength to forgive so I can move forward. Lord, reveal to me any areas of hurt and pain in my life—both those I remember and those I have forgotten. Heal my wounds and set me on Your path to victory. I love You, Lord, and want to be within the center of Your perfect will for my life.

> "I AM TRULY BEGINNING TO EMBRACE MY WOMANHOOD."

June 15, 2005

Lord, this morning on the way to the train station I had a wonderful revelation. You revealed to me that I was born a woman as part of Your perfect plan for my life. Thank You, Lord, for my womanhood! I can't imagine that a man could be as in love with You as I am as a woman. I am truly beginning to embrace my womanhood. I love the deep friendships that I am developing and the female sensitivity. I am beginning to look at men a little differently now, Lord. Thank You for healing me!

During this time of waiting for entry into law school, I did what was necessary on my job to make the career transition that I believed God had promised me. I advertised the position I held so someone else could take over my job when I went to school.

June 26, 2006

Lord, I have screened sixteen applicants to take over my job. I am trying to hire my replacement with a start date of July 15 so I can train this person before I leave. Lord, from my perspective, time is running short and options are running low. I don't have the letter confirming my acceptance into the UDC law school program that begins on August 7—the commissioned personnel center director is asking daily if/when I will be accepted into law school and I am trusting You to take care of all of this! You are going to work another miracle here for me and I am praising You now and forevermore! I love You, Lord, and I trust You with my life! I have such a peace about all of this and it is because You are faithful. You are my God. Lord, You are my atmosphere. Without You I have no life. You sustain me and strengthen me—because of You I have my being. You love me with a perfect and everlasting love—this I know full well and feel it in the center of my soul. I lay my head on Your chest—pressing my ear to Your breast, listening to the heartbeat of heaven—the source of all life and all that exists. You encompass me in Your tender and loving arms, safe and secure from all harm. Never let me go, Lord. I never want to move from this place—from within the security and love of You, the lover of my soul. Take me, Lord, and make me one with You. I lay at Your feet, Lord; order my steps, order my life, use me for the furtherance of Your kingdom.

July 2, 2006

I want to be more like You, Jesus. Today I dressed up for church; I want the outside of me to line up with Christ in me. Last Sunday I wore a skirt and this week I dressed like a lady again. I have been buying new clothes and today I bought new sandals. I want to look like a woman, walk like a woman and act like a woman. Lord, I want every part of my life to line up with what Your will for my life is. Help to transform me, Lord. You have rearranged my inner being, and now I desire my outer self to look like what Your will for my life is. Don't let me hide behind baggy men's clothing any longer. Lord, You formed me as a woman; teach me to walk in that wonderful plan You have for my life. Lord, I love You with all my heart, mind and soul and will serve You and worship You for all eternity.

Prior to this time, I did all of my shopping the in the men's section of department stores. I wore blue jeans, men's shirts and tennis shoes almost exclusively.

July 5, 2006

Lord, You are a most awesome God! I am amazed at Your perfect orchestration, how You expertly bring the pieces together and show me little by little Your master plan. Lord, You are strengthening my faith and stretching me. But, as usual, You are doing it in the most loving and compassionate way. You surround me with sisters who have more faith than me to encourage and support me as I metamorphose into the woman You want me to be.

Lord, here I am! Today I offered my job to someone and he accepted. It is one month to the day till law school starts...and still no letter confirming my acceptance. I love You—I trust You—and I wait expectantly for Your miracle. That the Creator of the universe would be mindful of me and my future absolutely boggles my mind, but I know that You have perfectly orchestrated every minute detail of my future and that gives me great comfort and peace. I pray that You keep revealing Yourself to me as I grow in my faith and absolute love for You. Lord, You have completely reformed me from the inside out and the outside in. Help me, Lord, to become a leader of excellence; give me courage to become a bold advocate for proclaiming Your majesty to believers and unbelievers alike. I will not be silent anymore! Lord, give me the wisdom and knowledge that I need to serve You with my unique gifts and abilities. Equip me for Your glory—for all honor and glory and power are Yours forevermore.

While I continued to trust God and move forward in my faith with outward steps toward what I believed God would do for me, I also had moments of uncertainty and fear that occasionally gripped my mind. I had to put those fears aside and hold on to the truth of God's Word and the inner peace I felt when considering what I truly believed God would do for me. He had already overcome a seemingly insurmountable obstacle that only He could have orchestrated: the agreement of the Admiral to allow me to go to law school once accepted, even though the officer assignment board recommended against it. So I had to trust God.

July 10, 2006

Lord, I am really struggling with waiting on You. I still haven't heard from UDC that I have been accepted into law school and classes begin in less than a month. Funding has to be set aside for my school by NOAA, a laptop computer purchased, and final plans made. When will I know, Lord? Should I call the school? What would You have me do? I want to be completely within Your will. If calling represents my weakness in trusting You, then I won't call. But if I need to do something to receive my blessing…Lord, reveal it to me. Lord, I need Your peace and Your wisdom to do the right things. Make known to me the plans You have for my life and strengthen me and my faith to walk the road You have laid before me. I can't do it alone, Lord—I need You to walk beside me and whisper instructions into my ear. Hold me, Lord, for I am tired and weak!

Redefining Relationship

During this time, Barb and I were still struggling to redefine our relationship toward each other. We had turned away from homosexuality and were trying to figure out how we were supposed to relate to each other. We were still living in the same house, attending church together and enjoying the same friends.

July 16, 2006

Lord, this evening Barb and I had a very difficult conversation. During our women's group, Barb shared with the group a powerful lineup of scriptures You placed in her heart to share about the journey she and I have been on this year as we separate and turn from homosexuality. Tonight she confronted me with trying to figure out why we have been bickering and not loving toward each other. I shared with her the turmoil I am feeling inside as I begin to see a new path that You have for me, which may include marriage someday. Lord, I am confused and in turmoil over the changes I am experiencing. I want to dress and look different on the outside to reflect the incredible changes that You have manifested on the inside of me. I have been buying new, more feminine clothes, wearing nail polish and perfume. I am beginning to see men in a different light and even am considering the possibility of dating and marriage. Men are beginning to flirt with me. But at the same time, I have a life set up with Barb—plans for the future, a house together, finances intertwined, our lives completely wrapped up together—and the thought of breaking that all apart is extremely overwhelming. Not to mention the stresses I am experiencing at work—hiring someone to replace me and not knowing if I have been accepted into law school. Lord, I know You say in Your Word that we are not given challenges larger than we can handle and I know I am not alone in any of this, but I feel that I am stretched to the limit. I don't want to hurt Barb in the least and change is difficult. I am a person of my word and feel that if I don't fulfill my promises to her then I have broken my word. She says she releases me of any promises I have made. Lord, this is all so overwhelming and confusing. I can't make any decisions without Your counsel. Please, Lord, lead me in Your will; don't allow me to say or do anything that would be against Your will for my life. Help me to go through this with grace, love and mercy. Teach me Your ways, O Lord. I am reminded of how, when I am in a prayer meeting and You want me to speak a word, You make my heart pound within my chest until I obey You and speak Your word. The other day when reading Your Word I came across a scripture in Jeremiah, which describes the exact thing I have experienced on more than one occasion: "My heart pounds within me, I cannot keep silent. For I have heard the sound of the trumpet…" (Jer. 4:19b NIV). Lord, I want to be obedient to Your will for my life. I want to be in the center of Your will. Please, Lord and Holy Spirit, make it crystal clear to me every step I should take. Give me the courage and boldness to deal with each day and not to shy away from conversation and truth that must be told. Keep my chin up and my eyes focused on Yours, Lord. Show me how to have compassion. Teach me love and how to walk in Your will every day. I love You, Lord, and I need Your strength. Increase my faith and hold me, Lord, as I grieve. Comfort and hold Barb as the two of us go through the emotional pain to come. Let us keep our eyes focused on You, Lord, and not hurt each other with the things we say and do. I need Your grace, Lord.

On July 16, 2006, Barb wrote the following email to her sister with a copy to me:

We have become very involved in a women's ministry at our church and after quite some time began to feel like we were being deceitful about our lifestyle and who we were to these women. Deb and I continued to seek GOD's Word and it was revealed to us that even our sleeping together (no intimacy) was a stumbling block and we should separate bedrooms. I can't even begin to tell you how painful this decision was for us. I moved my room to one of the smaller rooms and even though we were in the same house it was like a death. It was and still is very painful in so many ways. We went up and down with emotions but we both knew we could not turn back, we must keep moving forward.

Deb has been making some monumental changes in herself, beginning to seek out her feminine side that's been hiding away. She has truly blossomed into a beautiful woman. She started wearing more feminine clothes and shoes and the transformation is grand. However, our personal interaction with each other had started to deteriorate. We were cross with each other and this has been going on for a while. Last night we sat down and began to discuss it. What came out of that discussion was Deb was starting to move toward seeking male attention. A guy from church apparently has taken notice of her newfound womanhood and beauty and has been flirting with her. She is scared and unsure about all this new attention and doesn't quite know what to do but she feels like she will marry a man and begin a new life in the future. That means incredible changes in our lives and opens up a whole bunch of additional emotions and decisions that have to be made. Decisions around the house, do we stay together as roommates and wait to see if a knight in shining armor comes to whisk her away, does she begin dating and do you bring your date home and introduce him to your ex-gay partner? So as you can imagine we are a little topsy-turvy emotionally right now. I needed to share this with you even in this way because neither one of us knows what the next step will be.

Deb will be on her way to Norfolk, Virginia, today for the week. This will give us each time to process all this stuff. Nothing rash is happening at the moment but I wanted to prepare you before we get to the stage of "we are selling the house and splitting" and you have no idea what happened. Just keep us in your prayers and thoughts, that this all works out for God's glory!

Barb and I were each going through a grieving process of sorts as the reality of our situation was sinking in. We both began to realize that drastic changes would have to be made, that we couldn't live together forever and the future was uncertain.

July 18, 2006

Lord, keep my steps in the center of Your will for my life. I am not my own; You have bought me with a tremendous price and I am Yours, Lord. Help me to walk through the difficult emotions to come with Your strength. Help me to make Your choices and follow Your perfect will. Lord, I know You have already worked out every minor detail regarding my life and Barb's life. Lord, reveal to us Your perfect plan as we walk with our eyes focused on You. Don't allow us to make any rash decisions. Lord, this feels like a death and I need Your strength to get through the grieving process. Please place people in my path to help me get through this. I pray for Your comforting angels to be with Barb as she goes through the emotional pain. Reveal Your perfect plan to her as she tries to figure out what lies ahead. Lord, help each of us to focus on today and not worry about tomorrow. I love You and trust You completely, Lord.

July 23, 2006

Lord, what a powerful and mighty God You are! Thank You for the sermon this morning—it was written and delivered just for me. Thank You for strengthening my faith, Lord, as I continue to walk by faith and not by sight or might. Continue to use me; diminish Debora and increase Jesus in my life! Sensitize my spirit to demonstrate Your love in my life. Let me not focus my energy on things of this world; Lord, there is a spiritual battle in the heavenly realm that I need to be in tune with. It is not about the things of this world. You are testing me and teaching me while here on this earth so that I will be successful in life everlasting. Strengthen my courage and my faith, Lord. Let me be a bold witness to Your power and grace in my life. As I go back to work tomorrow to officially hand off my job to my replacement, let Your light shine through me that I may be a witness to him. Help me to smoothly hand over the reins as I prepare for law school and the next chapter of my life that You have already authored. For You are the author and finisher of my life—it is not my own—You bought me at an incredible price and I am now Yours. I stand at the threshold ready to step through a new door into a new chapter of my life. I pray that You bring the right people into my path and help me fulfill Your purposes for my life. You, O Lord, are my first love and will always be my highest love.

July 29, 2006

This past week was tough. I have had some very long days at work making the transition to hand over all of my duties and responsibilities. I also worked with the senior officers to identify funding for law school, but as You know, I still don't have the acceptance letter!

On Thursday of this past week one of the women from our women's group came to our house because she had a message for Barb and me. She began to read from Romans 1:24-27. She had misunderstood things that both Barb and I had said during various utterances of our testimony about the deliverance You have miraculously performed in our lives. She came here to tell us that You don't approve of our homosexuality! Lord, I really don't understand how she misheard or misunderstood what we said, but if she did, there are probably others who don't understand as well. We spent three hours with her giving her our entire testimony, assuring her that we are completely delivered. Lord, people can't see the deliverance from the outside and we need to tell people about Your wonderful work in our lives!

On July 31, 2006, I sent the following email to the dean of UDC Law School:

I currently hold a letter from you dated May 10, 2006, stating that I am on the waiting list for an opening in the JD class of 2009. I am excited about the opportunity to begin law school next week and want you to know how serious I am about the incredible opportunity to begin this new chapter in my life.

Two weeks ago I hired someone to replace me in my current job and I have announced to my employer and coworkers that this Friday will be my last day on the job. I am stepping out on faith that I will be admitted to UDC David A. Clarke School of Law to begin orientation next week.

Attached you will find a copy of the May 10th letter along with my completed registration forms and a funding commitment from my employer for the first semester's tuition. I have secured a laptop computer, meeting all of the requirements of the law school, completed my essay for the "Law and Justice" class, and purchased and am reading Faces at the Bottom of the Well by Derrick Bell to meet a reading requirement for the Lawyering Process course during orientation.

As you can see, I am ready to begin law school next week. I have done all that I can to prepare to take the next step toward fulfilling the destiny God has for my life. I sincerely hope that you will consider granting me the opportunity to register for classes next week and allow me to prove to you that I will be an asset to the UDC-DCSL both now and in the future. Sincerely, Debora Barr

August 2, 2006, email to my friends and prayer partners

God is SO AWESOME! I received a call from the Dean of Admissions at UDC law school late this afternoon and I have been admitted into law school! School starts next week. I have been on the waiting list since May 10th. For those of you who don't know, I have been believing God for this ever since the May 10th letter and actually hired someone to replace me at work. I have been training him for the past two weeks and announced to all of my coworkers that this Friday would be my last day at work since I would be going to law school next week.

"GOD IS SO AWESOME!"

Other than believing that God would work out the details, I had no letter in hand stating that. BUT GOD worked out the details and I will be going to school for the next three years (won't cost me a dime—and I will still get paid my full salary! AND I will have a job when I return as a lawyer!) how is that for working out details?

This was yet another powerful miracle in my life where God honored my faith in Him and He did not disappoint me! He is true to His Word. "For the eyes of the LORD run to and fro throughout the whole earth, to show Himself strong on behalf of those whose heart is loyal to Him" (2 Chron. 16:9). Is anything too hard for God? "Behold, I am the LORD, the God of all flesh. Is there anything too hard for Me?" (Jer. 32:27).

August 4, 2006

Lord, in James Your Word says, "For as the body without the spirit is dead, so faith without works is dead also" (James 2:26). I found this passage referenced in a book that I am supposed to read for one of my classes during orientation next week. It was confirmation that my actions on Monday were indeed what You required of me. Lord, You did it! You got me into law school!

August 6, 2006

Lord, You are so awesome! I am so proud to be a child of the Most High God! Abba Father, You are stretching me and growing me. I am listening to Your still small voice and obeying You. I shared my testimony about the awesome power and grace You have shown in my life with everyone I came into contact with today. Lord, every time I obey You, trust You and step out in faith, You honor that small step and bless me abundantly. I pray that You continue to use me for the furtherance of Your kingdom.

August 20, 2006

Lord, I continue to be excited and extremely thankful to You for my admittance into law school. I absolutely love the learning and this incredible change in my career. Help me to recognize the divine appointments along the way as You lead me on Your narrow path. I love You, Lord, with all my heart, all of my mind and all my soul and there is no other. Thank You for choosing me, loving me and blessing me. Help me be a blessing to others. Let Your light shine through me; clean out my heart and soul of anything not pleasing to You. Burn away the dross and never allow me to turn from You and worship idols of this world. May I continually sing Your praises and tell the world about You in my sharing of my testimony with anyone who will listen.

December 31, 2006

Lord, I thank You for this incredible year. The women's group meeting tonight was awesome. God, You are so awesome—I pray that You will continue to use me and enable me to share my testimony to Your glory. Lord, I owe You my life. I owe You my very existence and I desire to serve You with my whole heart, soul and mind in the upcoming year and into eternity. Please continue to feed me and teach me and refine me as I walk day by day closer to You. Jesus, You know the desires of my heart: to walk in Your will daily and to fulfill Your destiny for my life. Enable me to succeed and do well in law school. I pray that You will open new doors for me in 2007 and that You and I become closer and closer. Gently remind me who I am: a child of the Most High God, loved by the Creator of the universe. Lord, order my steps; show me the way to fulfill Your will for my life. Give me the courage to witness to anyone You place in my path this year. Give me boldness to speak of Your love and confront those who don't know You to tell them the good news of Your salvation and grace. I pray that You deepen and enrich my relationships and bring men into my life to bring balance. Flourish the fruit of my spirit in 2007!

CHAPTER 7

The New Beginning Years

(2006–2008)

Part II—2007

Therefore, if anyone is in Christ, [s]he is a new creation; old things have passed away; behold, all things have become new.

2 CORINTHIANS 5:17

January 1, 2007

New Year...new beginnings! Thank You, Lord, for 2006. What an awesome year of growth—spiritual growth and maturity. Thank You for Your Word and Your promises to us, Your chosen adopted daughters. In You I have hope for an eternal future and destiny in Your kingdom. I thank You for growth that has happened for myself and for Barb. Tonight we talked about the future and Barb said she knows that we will not be together forever, that we will have to move on in what destiny You have planned for us individually. Thank You, Lord, for preparing each of us to walk in Your will for our lives; You are such a gentleman in the way You move in our lives, never faster than we are ready.

March 7, 2007

Lord, You are moving in our lives once again. Barb and I have decided to separate physically because we believe it is Your will for our lives at this time. Barb is looking for a place to live and today we drew up a contract between us regarding the near-term agreements and plans for the eventual sale of this house and the splitting of the proceeds. We are grieving and looking forward at the same time. Big changes to stability are disconcerting and I am feeling very emotional over this. Lord, we continue to focus our eyes on You and hold on tight to You and Your promises to us. I pray for guidance and wisdom as I have been asked to share my testimony this Sunday as the pastor's message is on dying to self to gain life through You. Make clear to me how to tell what You have done in my life in a powerful message that will change lives for Your glory. I ask that You use me to further Your kingdom—give me Your words; place them in my heart and in my mouth so Your glorious message will be proclaimed. Lord, protect us with Your love and comfort us as we go through this difficult transition. We keep our eyes focused on Yours and know that You are moving us to the next level in You!

March 10, 2007

Lord, I know You are moving in a mighty way in our lives. Barb found an apartment and will be moving out on March 24th—two weeks from today. I feel like we are caught up in a whirlwind. Ever since You delivered us from homosexuality we kind of knew in the back of our minds that this day would come. We couldn't continue to live together forever and the day has come. Lord, cover us with Your wings and protect us through this emotional storm. God, I know You have great plans for us and are moving us up to the next level.

March 24, 2007

Lord, today is the day that You ordained as the first day in the next chapter of my life. It has been an emotional day and I am tired. I am just lying down to sleep. Barb is in her new apartment for the first night and I am in my house alone. We celebrated our new beginnings with our dear friends. The reality of what You are doing in our lives is truly sinking in right now. While we are excited about the incredible future You have planned, it is difficult as we grieve the loss of what we are giving up. Lord, following You is so hard! There are many tears along with the joy. Help me to be strong and give me Your words as we share and explain what You have done in our lives to both our saved and unsaved friends. Help us to give You the glory through every encounter we have with family and friends. Let Your love shine through, Lord! I pray for Your comfort and strength as I adjust to my new life. Hold me close, Jesus, as I feel that my world is rocking. Thank You for the dear friends You have placed in my life to hold me up and comfort me, pray for me and support me, Lord. I give You all the glory, honor and praise forever and ever. Amen!

THERE IS NOTHING IN THE WORLD LIKE KNOWING THAT YOU ARE IN THE CENTER OF HIS WILL.

Truly following Christ, taking up our crosses and following Him daily requires sacrifice. Sacrifice is painful at times, but oh so worth it in the end! There is nothing in the world like knowing that you are in the center of His will, knowing that what you are doing is pleasing in His sight.

April 8, 2007, Easter Sunday

Lord, as You know today has been particularly difficult and emotional for me and for Barb. We went to church together this morning and then we had lunch together at the house. She then left for her apartment so I could study. Today being a holiday where we normally invite ladies to our house for dinner, did not happen as in years past. We both felt isolated, lonely and abandoned. Lord, this is a difficult path that You have asked me to walk. I cried a lot today as I grieve the loss of familiarity and companionship. I was so sad and disjointed that I gathered up things to help Barb hang pictures in her new apartment and drove over there to spend some time with her. I feel like whenever we are here at the house the conversation is strained. I worry about her and her isolation and at the same time sometimes feel overwhelmed here alone with the responsibilities of the animals, house and property. I know it is not easy to die to self and follow You, Lord. I depend on You completely to be my companion and counselor.

This coming Saturday I will be sharing my testimony at a gospel concert. I pray that You continue to use my life and my scars for Your glory; give me Your words to speak, Your message for the people You have predestined to be there. May You receive all of the honor and glory through the testimony of my life. I love You, Lord, and place all of my concerns, pains and fears at the base of the cross to be washed in Your precious blood.

April 16, 2007

Lord, today was another difficult and emotional day for me. I feel so exposed after giving my testimony to a room full of people—some friends and many strangers. Now I feel uncomfortable in public, wondering if the people around me were there to hear the difficult parts of my life. I know that You were much more exposed on the cross than I will ever be—forgive me, Lord, for my weakness; please strengthen me. Today I didn't have to go to school because it's a holiday. I needed to stay home and heal my wounds. You ordained that holiday just for me, Lord. Thank You. Today I printed and addressed envelopes to mail our twenty-four testimony letters to our family and friends as we approach our seventh anniversary on the 22nd of this month. Lord, please stay close to me and hold me tight as I experience the emotions associated with all You are doing in my life. I stand empty and naked before You, asking You to fill me with Your anointing oil to overflowing. I ask You for Your blessing, Lord, over my life.

Friends and Family

In April 2007, Barb and I composed a message to send out to all of our closest family members and friends in the "gay community" that were a part of our social structure from the time we first met to the time we separated. This letter was difficult to write because for some of the people we sent it to, we had spent years convincing them that our life together was ordained by God and that we were born gay and could not change even if we wanted to. That letter is reproduced below.

Dear Friends and Family,

As many of you know, Barb and Deb have been seeking God and His truth for our lives. We have been studying His Word over the past four years and have come to know Him intimately. During this time we have held onto who we were, separately and together believing that God made us as homosexual women; that God loved us where we were, and that through relationships with people such as yourselves we could encourage you to love us and accept our lifestyle.

What we have come to realize over time is that God did not create us to live a homosexual lifestyle, that it was a deliberate choice we made and have now come to realize that it was never His plan for our lives. As we continued to seek Him and His purpose for us, we each discovered that our lifestyle was not pleasing to Him. He is a gracious and loving God and He has slowly transformed our lives in accordance with His will.

This has been a gentle transition over a period of two years—at first we discontinued our intimate relationship, then we moved into separate bedrooms in our home and now we live in separate homes. Deb still lives in the house and Barb has moved into an apartment. Deb plans to remain in the house until completion of law school and then we will consider selling the property.

Jesus tells us in His Word (Luke 9:23-27) to take up His cross and follow Him. This means to deny our flesh desires and follow Him in complete willingness and obedience. Following Christ is more important to us than anything this Earth has to offer.

Though we understand that you may be confused and sad for us, we ask that you not be. We have found complete Joy, Peace and Happiness! We are still the best of friends and will always be there for our friends and for each other. We are excited about the journey that we are on and we know that God has great plans for our lives! We are excited about how He will use us, and the story of our lives, for the glory of His kingdom. We pass no judgment on our friends and family who are living the lifestyle that we have chosen to walk away from. We have no right to judge anybody!

We will be praying for each of you, that God will shower His blessings on you, that He will give you peace and comfort and help you to understand and accept the great miracle that He has completed in our lives. If you don't know Jesus, we pray that you will come to know Him and if you do know Him, that you will come to know Him deeper than you can ever imagine!

With much love, Deb and Barb

The letter was received with mixed emotions. Some people contacted us and were happy for us and wished us well, but others did not understand. Some people even chose to sever ties with us.

April 20, 2007

Lord, I need You close to me tonight. I am experiencing strong emotions and I don't know if I am happy or sad. I received a call from our friend Carol today who called to tell me that she loves Barb and I and that she and her partner are here for us because they received our letter. Lord, I broke down when she called. I can't put my finger on all of the emotions but want to be strong for You, not allowing anyone to think that I regret this decision in any way. I don't know if I was just so relieved that she called and reaffirmed our friendship or if I am sad. I am feeling lonely and overwhelmed. I look at everything that needs to be done around here and get overwhelmed. I can't even keep the house clean, let alone mow ten acres—so much to do—and with law school, there's no time! Lord, I really need You right now, to hold me close and comfort me. I am feeling lonely and overwhelmed by everything that is happening in my life. Yesterday when I got off the train a lady walked up beside me and asked if I was the same person who spoke Saturday night at the gospel concert—one of my fears realized! That someone who was in the audience would recognize me after baring my soul and deep secrets to strangers! Thank You for the gentle encounter of encouragement. I was not judged or ridiculed. I also received a card from another lady encouraging me and telling me how much my testimony meant to her. I thank You, Lord, for these encouragers in my life. Hold me close, Lord, and give me strength to get through this difficult time.

In June, Clarise moved to Minnesota to work on her dissertation for her PhD. I, along with another lady, took over leading the weekly Women Who Worship God Bible study at our church. This new responsibility of co-leading the women brought me even closer to God as I prepared weekly lessons and activities for class. I was also at this time continuing to experience turmoil in my relationship with Barb while at the same time trying to survive my first year of law school.

July 8, 2007

Jesus, I need Your peace and comfort! I feel so lonely and out of sorts. I am trying to do what You want me to do and be who You want me to be and I can't seem to get it right! I am losing control! I am feeling like a total failure. I am not happy. I am lonely and afraid. Barb just left here angry and upset; she says I have erased her out of my life because I only have pictures up in the house of my family. Barb feels uncomfortable in what used to be "our house." I want to trust You Lord. I am not sure of myself—I am not sure I know what I am doing, trying to lead a women's ministry when I can't even get myself together, Lord. I need to feel You close to me. I need You to fill the void I feel in my life. I feel so lost and all alone! Jesus, please heal me; fix the broken areas of my life and help me to keep my eyes lifted up to You. Help me to hear Your still small voice. Love me, Lord—I am hurting!

July 11, 2007

I thank You for the time that Barb and I spent talking this evening. We were able to get some things out in the open about how we are feeling. I was feeling controlled by her and began to push her away. I felt like the enemy was attacking from every side. Help me, Lord, to keep my eyes focused on Your will. Barb and I discussed the house tonight and my desire to buy her out and keep the property. Lord, please make a way for me to make this happen and ensure she gets her fair share out of it. Lord, I totally trust You with my life.

God answered my prayer once again, making it possible for me to take out a second mortgage on the house so I could give Barb cash for her portion of the equity. I am convinced that every time we pray in accordance with His will, He answers our prayers and makes a way out of no way over and over again.

August 20, 2007

Lord, today I transferred the money to Barb's account to buy out her half of the property so she can purchase her own home. Thank You for providing a way for us to move forward legally and financially to sever the ties we set up when living a lifestyle not pleasing to You.

August 25, 2007

Lord, You continue to amaze me! Thank You for allowing me to serve You as You stretch me and push me gently outside my comfort zone until my comfort zone expands to fill the new and larger territory. You have been right beside me as I begin to speak more boldly about Your goodness and impact on my life. This week I was able to share my testimony with a couple of people at school; I know You expect me to continue to glorify You there. You have also given me a deep love for the people You have placed in my life and have given me an extra measure of compassion and care for them.

August 26, 2007

Lord, I feel like You are still healing me from past hurts. Last night I experienced something in my sleep that I also experienced a couple of nights ago. I woke up in the night during a heavy downpour of rain and realized I was crying—sobbing almost. Lord, I don't consciously know the work You are doing but trust You completely and surrender to You to complete Your work in me.

"I WOKE UP IN THE NIGHT DURING A HEAVY DOWNPOUR OF RAIN AND REALIZED I WAS CRYING..."

I feel like You are putting me on the front lines during the day, stretching me and pushing me outside my comfort zone to witness for You; and at night You are bandaging and healing my wounds, tearing away scar tissue and restoring me. I love You so much, Lord, that it is hard for me to put into words how much I really love You. I pray that You will continue to use me and equip me to do whatever You want me to do on this earth while I am here until I can be with You for eternity in heaven, my Savior and Redeemer!

September 17, 2007

Jesus, thank You for this time of singleness in my life. I was looking at it as loneliness, but now I can see that You are allowing me this time to heal and spend extra time with You. I have more time to study the Word and sit and enjoy worship music and to unwind and just be with You. If I was in a relationship right now it is possible I would be spending less time with You. Thank You for knowing what is best for me and for ensuring that You protect me from myself! I worship You, Lord! You are my rock and my salvation, my husband, lover of my soul and friend I can turn to at any time. Thank You, Lord, for loving me with an everlasting love. I am sold out to You, Jesus!

Trials at School

October 1, 2007 a.m.

Lord, please be with me today as I face a challenge at school that I know You have set before me. Today we begin the Bible study You laid on my heart as leader of the Christian Law Society (CLS) and today is the day I will share my testimony with those who will be there. As You know, I have been keeping a low profile and have not spoken to more than a few people about my past. There is a gay and lesbian group on campus with an outspoken voice and great visibility and I will be "coming out of the closet" so to speak in this small law school community today. May Your light shine through me today. Holy Spirit, take over when I share so that I reveal only what You would have me disclose and in a way that glorifies You, Jesus!

October 1, 2007 p.m.

Thank You for being with me today at the Christian law society meeting. I could feel the prayer covering of my brothers and sisters in Christ whom I asked to pray me through it. Holy Spirit, thank You for taking over my body, mind and spirit. I saw You work mightily today as questions were asked by students and You gave me the perfect response to allow them to see God in a new light. Thank You for the excitement building in those present for what the future holds for this organization and for what You are going to do in our lives as we fellowship with one another, building each other up and providing a safe haven for discovery of You. Work in the minds and spirits of those who were present today; cause them to think about You and Your Word; give them a fire and hunger to get closer to You; ignite Your Spirit within each of them to draw others to You.

October 31, 2007

Lord, today was an incredible day of somewhat mixed emotions. This morning Barb officially signed over the deed to the house to me, and my assumption of the entire loan is complete. The legal ties are being severed. I feel good about it and a bit sad at the same time. The next step is the dissolution of our civil union. Lord, please guide me on this path; have me speak to the right people to make this happen. Barb currently has a contract on a new house in West Virginia. Thank You, Lord, for taking care of each of us through this process. Thank You, Lord, for loving me and orchestrating the minute details of my life!

November 5, 2007

Lord, what a day! I am exhausted but need to get down in writing what happened today. First thing this morning I filed divorce paperwork at the courthouse to begin the dissolution of our civil union. I pray that Your hand be on this process and that it proceed smoothly.

At school, I experienced persecution today. I was approached by "Ben" of "Outlaw" [the Lesbian Gay Bisexual Transgender (LGBT) group at school] a couple of weeks ago to co-host a panel about faith and homosexuality where we planned to bring in a gay-affirming Catholic priest and my former pastor to open up discussions about homosexuality and Christianity. The rest of the members of Outlaw are violently opposed to allowing such a discussion to occur at school. In fact, many of the students along with their faculty sponsors promised to protest if it goes forward. One of the female members of Outlaw asked me to meet with her and Ben. I agreed to meet with them. This woman was outraged and hurled insults at me. I tried to reason with her and shared my testimony with her. I explained that I understand where she is coming from, how I once had similar views. I tried to reason with her and explain that all we proposed to do is present opposing views on an issue with love and let people decide for themselves what to believe. She became more and more upset and, with pure hatred in her eyes, told me she hates Christians. When I looked into her eyes, it was almost as though she was demon-possessed. Lord, I pray for the salvation of her soul; she is Your child, Lord, and I pray that You will reveal Your truth to her in love. Father, I am not afraid to fight for You, knowing that You are with me in the battle. You are a mighty, awesome and sovereign God! Thank You for using me on the battlefield today!

November 13, 2007

Lord, I can see Your hand guiding the preparation for Friday's meeting. Today Ben let me know that the Catholic priest is still willing to participate in the discussion on Friday. More controversy was stirred up today as members of Outlaw petitioned their faculty advisors to protest this event on the basis that it has nothing to do with law. I spoke to the Christian law society faculty advisor about this. I was reminded about the scriptures where Paul is all things to all people in the furtherance of the kingdom. I wrote an email to Ben reminding him that our constitution and laws are based on Christian principles and that to be an effective gay-rights advocate it is important to understand what Christians believe and to hear different views even within the Christian faith. Lord, I thank You for strengthening me and being with me today as I begin a three-day fast in preparation for my participation in this event on Friday. You are an awesome, mighty and sovereign God and I love You with all my heart, soul and strength. Who knows? Perhaps I have experienced all that I have experienced in my life for a time such as this—an opportunity to change lives by sharing my testimony in love? May Your will be done through me, Lord!

November 14, 2007

Lord, I thank You for Your Word! Clarise prayed with me this morning and said You gave her Psalm 37 and she thought it might be for me. I didn't read it this morning but opened my Bible to that chapter to read tonight. As You know, there was a complete turn of events today with regard to the event on Friday. After talking to Pastor Scott earlier today and getting excited about how this conversation would go on Friday, Ben sent me an email and said he wanted to cancel for Friday and perhaps reschedule for next year sometime because of the heightened controversy surrounding this event. Apparently some of the faculty (including one of my professors this semester and the mentor assigned to me for next semester) circulated a letter of protest. I talked to Ben on the phone and conceded that we should cancel for this Friday. I am disappointed and have been wondering if there was something I did wrong—did I push too far or reflect this event in the wrong light? I considered breaking my fast upon the news of this event being cancelled, but, Lord, I made You a promise and I will keep it. This is not the end of the matter. You placed me in this school at this time for the furtherance of Your kingdom. I thank You for Your work.

"PERHAPS I HAVE EXPERIENCED ALL THAT I HAVE EXPERIENCED IN MY LIFE FOR A TIME SUCH AS THIS..."

I read Psalm 37 tonight as I was getting ready for bed and this part jumped off the page: "Commit your way to the LORD; trust in him and he will do this: he will make your righteousness shine like the dawn, the justice of your cause like the noonday sun. Be still before the LORD and wait patiently for him; do not fret when men succeed in their ways, when they carry out their wicked schemes" (Ps. 37:5-7 NIV).

Thank You, Lord, for speaking to me through Your Word! For laying it on Clarise's heart to share this scripture with me this morning knowing that I would need to lean on it tonight. I pray, Lord, that You strengthen me and enable me to be still before You and wait patiently for You. As Barb reminded me earlier today, in the end, You win! Justice will prevail and the prince of darkness will be banished to hell for eternity. Lord, I pray for my classmates whose eyes are darkened. I pray that Your light will shine into their hearts and You will rescue them from the talons of evil. I praise You, Lord, for what You have done in my life. I praise You with all of the heavenly hosts and join in their chorus of praise and worship of You, most holy one—Ancient of Days, the author and finisher of my life and Savior of my soul! I love You with everything I am, Lord!

November 15, 2007

Lord, I thank You for standing with me once again in the face of opposition! Outlaw had an event today and ended up verbally bashing the Christian Law Society with many of the faculty members, the dean and numerous students present. One of the members of CLS came to me in the middle of what was escalating into a mini-riot to ask me to come and defend CLS. I did not go into the middle of that battle, as I didn't think it could serve any good purpose for me to show up in the middle of a heated discussion. As it turns out, the professor whom I have for one of my classes this semester was the lead instigator! I confronted her after my class today and asked to speak to her about this whole issue and how it came to fruition. She agreed to meet with me next week. Lord, I pray that You prepare me for that meeting. I only want to please You, Lord, and glorify You through my life. Use me, Lord, for Your purposes. Protect me with Your armor and equip me with Your Word. This battle is not against flesh and blood; it is a spiritual battle. I know that full well. Steady my heart when it is pounding and slow my breathing as I face my giants in this battle. Shine Your light through me and use me for Your kingdom work.

November 20, 2007

Lord, I met with two gay female professors (my current professor and my assigned mentor for next year) today about the controversy surrounding the event Ben and I had planned for last week. I really feel that I let You down and didn't do an adequate job discussing this issue with them. I don't believe I said enough about Your love and was not intelligent with my responses to their pointed questions. I feel like I lost ground instead of holding ground or advancing forward. They really didn't want to hear my testimony; they said it was not at all relevant to the conversation. They asserted that there is no legitimate place in a public school for any organization asserting religious views and I made no good rebuttals to that stance. I feel like I failed! I could come up with no good reason why this idea should even be discussed at school. Lord, where were You with all I had planned to say? Once again when placed in a confrontational setting I caved in and let them walk all over me. I am not eloquent of speech, nor am I quick to be able to respond to verbal challenges. I showed my weakness in this area. I don't feel like I honored You. I am disappointed with the way the whole meeting turned out. Lord, I pray that I have not hindered Your purposes or thwarted Your plan. I am sorry for not doing better, for not saying the right things, for not standing my ground and for letting them get the upper hand. I pray that You will forgive me for my failure.

I truly felt that I had failed God by not defending my faith. I also did not know enough about the Constitution to intelligently argue why it was permissible to discuss issues of religion and faith in a public school. God reminded me that it is never my responsibility to defend Him. He doesn't need our help. I know what I believe and I know how He has changed my life, and I stood up to hostile opposition and defended my faith. I made an attempt to share my testimony of God's grace in my life, and that is all God required of me on that day. In hindsight, I think the professor who would become my advisor/mentor the following semester actually developed some respect for me that day. She was later one of my advocates, writing letters of recommendation for me after law school when I was seeking employment as a lawyer.

December 7, 2007

Today is my final exam in family law and this past week has been active in my own family law issue! On Saturday of last week I received an order from the family court dismissing my case for dissolution of the civil union. I have either fourteen days to appeal to the Supreme Court of West Virginia directly or thirty days to appeal to the Circuit Court. I plan to get a lawyer now.

I was concerned about the potential of this issue going before the Supreme Court of West Virginia, with all of the publicity that it would generate. I was still a commissioned officer and did not want my face and my personal life plastered in the news. I could envision the headlines: "Lesbian Couple Attempts to Undo a Vermont Civil Union in the Supreme Court of West Virginia."

December 10, 2007

Today Barb moved into her new house. I also hired a lawyer to help with the dissolution of our civil union. I never would have believed I would be saying these things three years ago! I am amazed at what You have done in our lives. I praise You, Lord, for Your mercy and Your grace.

CHAPTER 8

The New Beginning Years
(2006–2008)
Part III—2008

Therefore, if anyone is in Christ, [s]he is a new creation; old things have passed away; behold, all things have become new.

2 Corinthians 5:17

January 1, 2008

Lord, I thank You for 2007 and for strengthening me as I move into 2008. I just opened my letter to You written one year ago today. I pray You are proud of me, Lord, as I grow in the knowledge of You. Strengthen me this upcoming year. I pour myself out on Your altar to be filled with Your anointing oil. Replace everything in my life that is not pleasing to You with Your light and Your Spirit. Teach me to be a good leader; empower me to bring Your people closer to You, to spark in them the desire to know You more. Help me to be a good steward of the resources You have blessed me with. Empower me to give of my time, talents and resources to advance Your kingdom. Help me to pay off debt so I can give more freely. Speak clearly to me about career direction; help me make wise choices about my future and keep my feet in the center of Your path of righteousness. Teach me the depths of wisdom from Your Word. Keep me in the Word and in daily prayer. Teach me to pray effectively, to intercede for others more effectively, to connect to Your Spirit. Give me a holy boldness to speak boldly about You and Your salvation. Help me to overcome my insecurity and shyness when it comes to speaking to others about You, Lord. I love You, Jesus!

January 6, 2008

Lord, I praise You! What an incredible day! I attended both church services this morning because I just couldn't get enough of Your presence. The worship songs spoke to my heart, including "Let My Life Song Sing to You" and I felt Your strong presence during communion. As You know, I've been feeling very lonely now that Barb has moved from her apartment into her new house and has taken her dogs that I was watching—all except Sierra. I can't seem to disconnect from her as I feel I should. I've also been feeling unworthy of any position of leadership in the ministry and the enemy has been trying to reaffirm my doubts and fears—but You couldn't have gotten the message across to me any clearer if You had put a billboard up in my front yard with neon signs and lights today. At the second service a young lady from my women's group gave me a beautiful gift: a beautiful, hand-painted cross necklace. She said as soon as she saw it she thought of me and wanted me to have it. I put it on and have been looking down on it all day, and when I wear it and look down at it I see You clearly on the cross—every detail of Your body—arms, legs, head hung down and even the placard above Your head. When I took it off tonight and looked at it in my palm, all I could see was green ivy and purple flowers (not what I could see before). I put it back on my chest and looked down again and I can see You clearly. Absolutely amazing and so precious to me! Thank You, Jesus, for revealing Your sacrifice to me in such a tangible way! Thank You for loving me so much to give me this sign of Your love!

After church I went to the store to buy groceries and stopped at a restaurant for lunch. I was alone standing in line when a man from church invited me to sit with his family. Again, You are reaching out to show me that I am not alone. I am a member of Your family and will never be alone.

When I got home and walked Sierra before heading back to church for our women's ministry meeting, I was praying for Your wisdom and guidance and was sharing with You my doubts and fears about not being a good leader of the women and feeling inadequate. I received a phone call from a woman who wants to add people to the prayer list for tonight. I struggle with what to say to people when they are hurting and I still feel uncomfortable praying for people I don't know. As I headed to church for our women's ministry meeting, I again began to doubt. I thought nobody would show up for the teaching, but You brought twenty-six women to the meeting! Incredible! And what power in the sharing! Please continue to strengthen me and help me overcome my feelings of inadequacy. Give me wisdom to lead Your women.

To top it all off, I received a call from Clarise tonight from Minnesota and she had a message from You about Joshua and how he felt after Moses had died and he was left to lead the Israelites into the promised land. Thank You for all of the powerful messages today! I love You, Lord, with all my heart, mind, soul and strength and will serve You all the days of my life and into eternity! I will be a priest for You, Lord;

equip me for the work You have for me. I am willing and able; You are my Lord and Savior, El Shaddai, and I adore You! I join all of the heavenly hosts in praising You! Amen!

January 16, 2008

I talked to my lawyer today and the complaint will be filed in the District Court to ask the judge to dissolve our civil union. Lord, I pray Your will be done in this matter. I pray that it can be resolved at this level and not be elevated to the Supreme Court of West Virginia. Your perfect will be done—I trust You, Lord, knowing that You see the big picture. So whatever the outcome, I will do what You tell me to do. I have been re-reading THE PURPOSE DRIVEN LIFE and can see how that book and study planted seeds in my soul that have germinated and grown! It is so interesting to read the lessons in the book and see the statements and concepts that I hear myself repeating and teaching others. It is amazing how You have worked in my life, to pull me out of the miry pit of sin and set my feet on solid ground. I love You, Lord, with all my heart, mind and soul!

January 21, 2008

Jesus, I ask for Your peace and comfort for Barb. Today, I received the papers from the lawyer to have them served on Barb to try to get the judge to sever our civil union. I asked Margaret to serve the papers and she agreed. Barb shared with me tonight on the phone that she is upset about this whole process and feels like I am pushing really hard to sever these ties. She is upset about my unraveling our finances and closing the joint accounts and cell phone contracts and the other aspects of our "married" life. Help me, Lord, to be sensitive to her feelings and to be careful how I portray this dissolution. She said she will not interfere with the process. Father, I pray for Your blessing on this entire process, that You will prepare the judge to make a decision in accordance with Your will. Keep me in the center of Your will; direct my steps; guide my mind; filter my words and bless Barb as she moves forward in Your will as well.

February 10, 2008

Lord, I am not sure what to say other than to talk to You about yesterday. Barb and I went to a movie and dinner and the whole time seemed strained. I cried half of the time at dinner and came home and went straight to bed. I don't understand the dynamics and can't articulate my feelings. She wants to spend more time with me and I'm not sure I want that. I felt like I was sacrificing time that I really needed to use for study and she was talking about how a half a day just wasn't enough; that we need to schedule a whole day once a month. Lord, I pray that You reveal to me the root of the feelings I am having and to heal these areas of pain in me. I can't articulate my feelings and don't know what to do other than to ask You to heal me.

"LORD, I DON'T KNOW WHAT TO DO OTHER THAN TO ASK YOU TO HEAL ME."

February 14, 2008

Lord, I pray You direct the paperwork that is currently going through the court system regarding dissolution of my civil union. I pray that You direct the actions of the judge who will make the decision. I pray that You direct this matter in accordance with Your will.

February 18, 2008

Lord, I need Your guidance and direction to make the right decision. Barb and I have been experiencing very strained conversations and awkwardness around each other. We have been fighting a lot lately. She proposed an ultimatum today: that we either completely sever our ties and go our own ways or try to restore a level of friendship that is greater than what we have now. We both realize the impact this decision will have on a lot of people we care about. She is having great difficulty with my pulling away and apparent lack of time to spend with her. At the same time, I struggle every day because she is the first person I want to call with any news—just to stay in touch. I can't have it both ways. Lord, don't let me make any emotional/rash decisions. Speak to me and to Barb with Your will for our lives. Lord, I don't want to hurt her. I don't want to strain any relationships with our friends and church family. I don't know how to deal with this!

February 19, 2008

Lord, I just got a call from the lawyer to inform me that the judge signed the order to dissolve our civil union (on February 14th—the exact day I prayed to You to direct the judge in accordance with Your will). Thank You for answering my prayer to complete this quickly and easily without having to go to the Supreme Court. I have mixed emotions right now as I try to write through tear-filled eyes. I know this is Your will and I know what I have to do with regard to the question Barb asked yesterday. Lord, I need Your strength to be honest with her and to talk to her in love. Please prepare her heart and my words to be delivered and received with love. God, this is so hard! Please be with me through it all.

God sometimes answers our prayers even before we utter them—this He proved to me with the dissolution of my civil union. "It shall come to pass that before they call, I will answer; and while they are still speaking, I will hear" (Isa. 65:24).

Alone and Lonely

February 23, 2008

Lord, this is so hard! I met with Barb today and gave her the letter I wrote this week. I promised to stay away from her and respect the boundaries needed for healing. The finality of all of this makes me very sad. I am feeling very lonely right now. Lord, I know I am walking in Your will and I need to feel You close to me more than ever before. I pray that You will be with Barb and comfort her especially tonight. Surround her with Your love and let her know how much You love her. May Your peace flood over her and comfort her through this healing process. Help me to be strong and not to reach out to her in any way so she can heal. Lord, please be with me tonight and especially tomorrow as I have to face so many people who will want to know what is going on. Help me to be strong. I love You, Jesus.

February 29, 2008

Lord, as You know, this has been an extremely emotionally exhausting week for me. It started on Monday with Barb sending me an email demanding that I read and not delete it. The next day she began calling and leaving me voice mail messages threatening to show up on my doorstep if I don't make contact with her. I sent her an email and asked her to please stop trying to communicate with me. I feel like I am being pursued from all sides by the enemy. I need Your armor and Your protection, Lord. I love You with all my heart, soul and mind, and I want to be in Your will. I don't want to lash out in anger or with hatred. I need Your hedge of protection around me as I heal.

March 16, 2008

Lord, I thank You for this past week—spring break—healing and newness of life. I have struggled this past week with emotions—Barb resumed attempts to contact me early in the week. She doesn't understand why we can't be friends again right now and resume communication with each other. I need time alone and away from my emotional dependence on her. I need to be completely independent and strong in my own independence before I can resume a safe friendship with her. I have experienced ups and downs this week as I struggle to stay the course. I thank You for spring and the changing season. May this season's change bring spiritual growth to me and those under my care in ministry. Fill me with Yourself, Lord, so the thoughts I think are Your thoughts and the words I speak are Your words. Take over my life and renew me in You. I pray for comfort and peace for Barb. Heal the hurts and restore her, Lord. Thank You for Your grace and mercy and love.

March 25, 2008

Lord, thank You for loving me and watching over me. I know You are there all the time. I have been struggling with my emotions, especially around my separation from Barb. I haven't spoken to her since March 9 and it has been difficult. I felt like I needed a complete separation until I can heal and get on with my life—not depending on her for anything, for moral support, etc. It has been difficult, seeing her email me and call me and me not responding.

March 26, 2008

Jesus, I am so lonely! I need companionship. Evenings are the toughest! I come home to an empty house and run the same routine over and over. I miss having someone to talk to and share my thoughts with. I don't want to be single! Lord, I have done every tough thing You have required of me: I walked away from a lifestyle of sin and turned my life around. Now, all I have is loneliness! An empty house! I watch the people around me going home to their families and I want a family of my own. Help me, Lord, to be patient and wait on Your perfect timing as You direct my steps. Lord, I pray for Your love to fill the void in my heart. Your will be done in my life. You are sovereign God—the Ancient of Days—who formed the foundations of the universe; who always was, who is and is to come; the lover of my soul; my Creator; my Redeemer whose perfect will be manifest in my life. Forgive me, Lord, for crying out in desperation. Hold me, Jesus; let me feel Your arms around me. I love You, Lord!

"JESUS, I AM SO LONELY! I NEED COMPANIONSHIP."

March 31, 2008

Jesus, I need Your guidance and direction. I received an email from Barb today asking that we end this separation and resume our friendship. What would You have me do, Lord? What is Your will? I have been experiencing depression and loneliness but don't want to resume a relationship with Barb that is unhealthy. I want to rely on You and not her or any other person for fulfillment and completion. I don't want to be controlled by her or anyone else. I do want male companionship in my life. I don't want to feel pressured by anyone. Speak clearly to me, Lord, so I know what Your perfect will is.

While Barb and I had been separated and living apart for more than a year, there were still remnants of the emotional and relational ties that are woven together in any relationship between two people who have fallen in love and have been physical with each other. When God revealed to us that we were living outside His will for our lives, we were still the best of friends and loved each other very much. This was not a case of two people falling out of love with one another. Our decision to separate and live our lives in accordance with God's best for us took a strong act of our wills and a firm determination not to go back to the life we had together. God was still working with each of us individually to bring healing. He was also about to help me even more by bringing a greater separation in physical distance between the two of us.

Moving On...Literally

April 10, 2008

Lord, I sense You are on the move in my life once again. I attended a speed-mentoring program at a law firm in the city this evening. I am beginning to fall in love with the District of Columbia and have a desire to move there soon. I feel like it is time for me to move. I am excited about my future and what You have in store for me. Lord, You know the desires of my heart and You know what is best for me. I place my life and my future in Your hands. Lord, guide me on Your path.

April 17, 2008

Lord, I feel that You are doing a new thing in my life. I am preparing to move to the District of Columbia (D.C.). The word I have from You is "get ready." I am mentally preparing for the move and I am getting this property ready to sell. I am in contact with a real estate agent in the D.C. area to start looking. Help me, Lord, to overcome my fears and help me to let go of the material things that I love, including this beautiful house and property. Make the path smooth for me and direct my steps in the middle of Your will. Help me to make right decisions in accordance with Your perfect will for my life.

April 26, 2008

Jesus, I need Your reassurance that I am doing the right thing in preparing to sell my house. I am sitting in my bed tonight as the rain pours down feeling very lonely and unsure. I interviewed two realtors today and have an appointment to interview another on Monday to choose one to list this house for sale. I think I am moving in accordance with Your will, but at the same time I am grieving the loss of this house and property that I love and have cared for over the past seven years. This move is full of unknowns and I am nervous. It will result in my tearing away from my church family, my ministry there, people and places I know and love here in West Virginia and the start of something new and completely unknown: city life; smaller living space; new friends; a new church and a new life. I need to know for certain that this is what You want me to do before I can put this house on the market. I know that if I am walking in Your will You will provide for me. I know from Your Word that You will provide increase for me and will not allow me to be harmed. Lord, make it clear to me what You want me to do. Bring a buyer quickly and open the doors for me to get a new home that I will love in a city I will love. Give me a new ministry, a new church, so I can glorify You through my testimony. Lord, I am counting on You to provide my every need. Make all decisions for me. Open doors I am to walk through and close all doors that I force open outside of Your will. Protect me, Lord, as I rest in the shadow of Your wings. Jesus, I give You complete authority to make every decision related to my future. I won't take a single step in any direction without You telling me where to go. Help me, Lord, to take each and every thought captive and to line it up with Your will for my life. I don't want to be in control of my future—You are the Lord of my life! May You be glorified in everything I do; may Your love, mercy and forgiveness be my testimony to each person I meet in this life transition. May my life be a witness for You. Your glory being revealed is what I commit my life to. I love You, Jesus!

May 16, 2008

Lord, the house and property are ready to go on the market tomorrow. I thank You for giving me the opportunity to inhabit this incredible home and to care for this beautiful property. I ask Your blessing on this place as You bring the new caretakers here and it is handed off to the new owners. I thank You in advance for my new home and my new life in D.C. I pray that You ease the fears and sorrow of my friends as they prepare for my departure. I pray for favor as You transition me and usher me into the next level in You. Jesus, I trust You completely and place my life and my future in Your hands. Guide me along the path You have set out for me. Help me to see the doors You are opening to my future. Speak clearly, Lord, so I don't miss Your still, small voice. Guide me on Your path of righteousness and truth—use me to advance Your kingdom. Here I am, O sovereign Lord, ready, willing and able to go where You want me to go and to do what You want me to do. I praise You, Lord! I love You, Lord! Amen!

May 17, 2008

Jesus, I put my house on the market today and am a little nervous and sad. I am nervous about the uncertainty of what lies ahead and sad to know I will be leaving this incredibly beautiful home and property. I ask for Your comfort tonight, Lord. Please hold me and reassure me that I am doing the right thing, that I am truly hearing Your voice and following Your will for my life. Help me to be certain You are here with me, Jesus. This is really hard, Lord.

It was very difficult for me to put the house on the market to sell. Barb and I had designed and built our dream home together (a custom log home) on a large piece of land with privacy overlooking a beautiful view of mountains off in the distance. It was cozy, had a big fireplace, large glass windows, a large front deck that spanned the entire length of the house and an open floor plan. I had created a beautiful garden with flowering plants, many bird feeders and a pond in front of the house, and had planted nearly twenty trees on the property. I absolutely loved the seclusion and privacy of the property. It was my refuge. I had an old 1952 antique farm tractor that I mowed the property with, and I just loved being outdoors as much as possible. Knowing that I was about to give all of this up for the uncertainty of life in the city was unsettling. But I knew from experience that following God's will for my life always results in increase. What I was about to give up would be replaced and increased in some way; I just knew it!

I KNOW FROM EXPERIENCE THAT FOLLOWING GOD'S WILL FOR MY LIFE ALWAYS RESULTS IN INCREASE.

June 23, 2008

Lord, I believe You are once again moving on my behalf regarding the sale of my home. Saturday I received a call alerting me that someone wanted to look at the house. That evening the realtor called with a bunch of questions and came to walk the property lines with me. I pray that You facilitate this deal and smooth my transition to my new home. I love You, Lord. Thank You for working out every detail of my life.

July 1, 2008

God, You are so amazing! I can't begin to describe how much I love You and am thankful for every detail of Your concern for me! While praising and worshipping and praying on the way home from school, I asked You to bring buyers for the things I am advertising for sale in preparation for my move and You had already answered my prayer before I prayed it! Two voice mail messages on my home phone from this afternoon with people who were calling to purchase items I have for sale. I also know You are working with the buyer who looked at my property two weekends in a row. I just love You so much, I feel my heart will burst! I thank You for our early morning walks and for Your hand in my life.

July 7, 2008

Lord, thank You for continuing to work out the details of my life! I am moving forward with looking at homes in D.C. I love You and trust You completely. Without You I have no life. In You I have my life and breath and being. I so much want to get out of here as soon as possible and put my past behind me.

On Saturday Barb and I were sitting on a bench downtown eating ice cream cones after she helped me sell things at the flea market, and a group of gay women from our previous circles came along to talk to Barb. I felt SO uncomfortable! I just wanted to run and shout at the top of my lungs, "This is not what it looks like!" I so much want to put my past behind me. Please, Lord, hurry up and get me out of here!

July 9, 2008

Lord, thank You! I got a call from the realtor today and my buyers are coming out again this Saturday. I know they will make an offer on the house. I am so excited that You are working out the details. I have scheduled an appointment with my D.C. realtor on Tuesday to look at condominiums in the District. I will be moving this summer! You are so awesome, God! In this terrible housing market You sold my house and moved mountains on my behalf. I love You, Lord, and am so excited to see what You have for me in my new life in D.C.

July 12, 2008

Lord, You have done it again. I praise You, Lord, for all You are—the Ancient of Days and the lover of my soul. I just found out that I have an offer on the house, but I won't get to see it until tomorrow morning. You are so faithful. I pray that it is an offer I can accept and move on with my plans for moving at the end of the month. Thank You, Jesus, for confirmation and for increasing my faith even more.

July 13, 2008

Lord, I saw the offer on my house today; they came in $50,000 less than the list price and want me to include the tractor and four-wheeler at no charge! God, I felt You wanted me to counter with my break-even price: $30k off the list price. I pray, Lord, that You facilitate this contract to completion. I trust You, Lord, and whatever happens I will continue to praise You and trust You. I surrender everything I have and everything I am to You, Lord. I am completely in Your hands.

When the offer came in on my house and I didn't know what to do, I called Jayne, an older and wiser woman of God whose advice I valued and trusted. She assured me that when making important decisions such as this, I will always know the will of God when I have peace in my heart about a particular decision. She told me that God's way is peace. If there was any unsettling or anxiety when deciding one thing over another, that is not the will of God, and I should walk away. When I met with the realtor the next day and prayed about the offer/counteroffer on my house, I made my decision to sell based on the peace I felt in my heart.

July14, 2008

Lord, it is done. I signed the contract today to sell my house. I am now on the path to my future and my new life in D.C. The closing date is August 28. I am taking a huge loss on the house and actually have to bring money to the table to close along with giving up the tractor and four-wheeler at no cost to the buyers. It now appears that I may not be able to buy a house in D.C. since I don't have any money to put down on a loan. Perhaps I am to rent? Only You know, Lord, and I ask You to speak loudly and clearly to me and make all decisions for me. I had such a feeling of peace about the final deal that I believe I am doing what You want me to do. I am trusting You, Lord, to take care of me through it all.

July 15, 2008

God, You are so awesome! I am absolutely amazed beyond my wildest imagination about what You did for me today. I am sitting here with the contract for my new condo in D.C.! It was the first one I looked at today and I fell in love with it. It has everything I have been asking You for and more. You moved mountains on my behalf today and allowed me to purchase a new home that meets all of my needs with absolutely no money down because You know I depleted my cash reserves in the sale of my home in West Virginia. I wish there were words in some language I could speak to express how much I love You and how grateful I am that You love me so much! Give me the language, Holy Spirit, to convey my gratitude and love to the Father, I pray!

I spent the rest of the summer taking long walks by the river every morning, praying and communing with God in nature. I knew my life was about to change dramatically. Soon, I would no longer live in the country where I could spend a lot of time outdoors, which I absolutely love; rather, I would be in the city and unable to walk outside into nature every single day. God spoke to me and encouraged me when I spent quality time with Him in prayer.

July 16, 2008

Lord, I don't want to forget what You spoke to me about on our walk by the river this morning. You showed me how my experiences and emotions are somewhat parallel over the past three days or so to what Your disciples must have experienced at Your death and resurrection. You entered Jerusalem amid praise and celebration—like my finding out that the buyers were making an offer on my house and the celebration and excitement I felt over that, which soon turned to fear and apprehension as I waited for word of the offer—then, much the same as the disciples watching You being crucified, finding out that the offer seemed impossibly bad, something I could not accept. There was then mourning and fear over my sending a counteroffer and worrying about whether they would accept or walk away; then the glorious resurrection of coming to an agreement and completing a contract—although I believed it would be impossible for me to buy a new home with no cash—then to see the miracle You performed yesterday better than I could ever hope or imagine: much like the disciples seeing You resurrected. Thank You for showing this to me.

"I WANT A NEW IDENTITY AND I WANT TO EMBRACE MY FEMININITY."

July 19, 2008

Lord, You are still answering my prayers and forging a path for me. On my walk with You this morning I told You that I want a new identity and that I want to embrace my femininity, which requires new clothes, a new walk, a new way of seeing myself. Then tonight I got a call from Kay, who wanted to know if I would be interested in clothes and shoes she was getting rid of! Thank You, Lord! I praise You for hearing and answering my prayers.

August 7, 2008

God, Your love for me is absolutely amazing! This morning as I walked with You in the cool of the morning by the river I began to pray in the spirit and Your presence came over me just as You did one night last week: my chest cavity filled so full of You I could feel Your physical presence and love for me. God, I want so much more of You! I want to feel Your presence so tangibly in my life! I want to walk with You as Enoch walked with You. I want to see Your face and speak to You as Moses spoke to You. I want to see and witness Your power as Moses did. I want to stand next to You, Jesus, and see You raise the dead and heal the sick and deliver the brokenhearted. God, use my life, use my body, use my voice, use my hands; let me see with Your eyes, let me hear with Your ears; teach me, Lord, to live in Your presence, to live in Your power. Use everything I have, Lord, and I pray, Holy Spirit, that You will expand my prayer language because I have so much to thank and praise God for that I need 10,000 tongues to communicate my love and adoration of Adonai!

August 9, 2008

Lord, thank You for what You revealed to me on our walk to the river this morning. As I was looking up into the tall trees of the forest, the sun was beginning to come up enough to illuminate the treetops and begin to filter down. You showed me that as Your Word enters my mind (the top), it enters my DNA and changes me—it brings life and nourishment to my soul. Without it, there is no life. Light is necessary for a tree to breathe and have life just as Your Word and my internalizing it is necessary for my spiritual life. Thank You for this revelation! Continue to teach me, Lord, and strengthen my spirit so I can draw others to You through my witness.

August 18, 2008

Lord, I thank You for walking with me this morning. I love our private time together. You showed me this morning that I am less than two weeks away from a new season in my life. Labor Day weekend marks the end of summer and that is when I will be moving to D.C. I am feeling a bit overwhelmed in this last week before school starts with packing up this house and doing everything necessary for the move. Thank You for working out the details for me, Lord!

August 21, 2008

Lord, I am struggling with emotions today! I went to D.C. today to pay for my fall tuition and to meet the realtor at the condo for the home inspection. I realize now that I still have too much stuff to move into this very small condo. I am used to having plenty of space and have accumulated a lot of things. I know I will adjust. I am just feeling overwhelmed by the details that still have to be worked out. Help me, Lord, to trust in You and to rest in Your peace.

August 24, 2008

Lord, I made it through the whole day today without crying but now that I am home alone on the last Sunday in this house...the tears are falling. I just finished the last thank-you card for the party that was thrown for me by my friends yesterday. Help me to experience Your power in my life especially as I move into this new season You have for me. Help me, Lord, to be a shining and bold witness for You. I am sad to leave the closeness of my friends and sisters in Christ who have become my family, and my church, which has become my home, and the home that symbolizes my past and new beginnings. But I am also excited to see what You have in store for my future because I know that with this move You are taking me to the next level in You. I give myself to You completely, Lord—all that I am is Yours—use me for Your glory, direct my steps, speak through me, transform me into the perfect image of Your Son Jesus Christ. Holy Spirit, take over every aspect of my life; transform me completely; burn away every impurity so that the Father can use my life for His purposes.

August 26, 2008

Lord, it is my last night in this house…the dream house that Barb and I built together almost eight years ago. I am exhausted emotionally and physically as I have been packing and coordinating for weeks to make this move to D.C. When I stop long enough to sit down—like now—it makes me sad to leave this beautiful house and land, my friends and my church family. With school already started and with my daily treks back and forth from D.C., my mind has been fully occupied. Lord, help me to focus on You and to rest in Your peace these next few days as I go to D.C. for class tomorrow morning and return to West Virginia to rent a moving truck and pack up the house in the truck. Thursday morning I go to settlement on this property and the condo in the evening. Lord, please give me the strength and stamina to get all of this done.

I made that move with the help of some friends over the Labor Day weekend.

September 1, 2008

Lord, today turned out to be a tough day for me. I keep getting lost trying to navigate around the city. My friends have been calling to check on me and pray for me. I am feeling like a fish out of water here. It is so different from what I am used to and I am out of sorts. Lord, help me to reconnect intimately with You. I feel like I am in survival mode and can't seem to relax and talk to You. I don't feel completely safe when I walk outside here. At one point today I just collapsed into a chair and the song came on the radio: "Be still and know that I am God." Thank You for letting me know You are right here with me through these tough times and through my tears. I love You, Lord, and want to please You. I know that You have placed me here in D.C. and I am where I am supposed to be. Strengthen and comfort me, Lord. Help me rest in Your arms and not try to do this on my own.

Right or Wrong Decision?

September 7, 2008

Lord, this week has been one of highs and lows for me as I am settling into my new environment. I have been feeling overwhelmed with school and life. I am not completely comfortable in this neighborhood; I witnessed men being arrested yesterday morning when I was walking Sierra. Police have been setting up floodlights a block from my house at night and it appears there is an awful lot of police activity around here, making me very uneasy. Lord, I pray for Your protection and ask that You make me streetwise in a hurry! I want to find a church and get connected to a body of believers as soon as possible. Lord, I miss the closeness I felt with You over the summer on our long walks by the river. Please make Your presence known to me and felt by me as I am struggling with the unfamiliarity of absolutely everything in my life right now. Please protect me from all harm and watch over me. I know You told me to move to this city and opened every door to make it happen. I obeyed You, Lord. I sold my house; uprooted my life; and left my support structure, friends and familiar surroundings to move to D.C. I have never lived in a city like this, never lived in a condo, don't really know my way around and am not sure why I am here!? Lord, I pray that You speak to me; guide and direct me; fill me with Your Spirit daily and draw near to me. I love You, Lord, and trust You with all my heart, mind and soul.

September 7, 2008

God, I see it now. I am reading WALKING WITH GOD by John Eldridge and just read the section about recognizing and praying against spiritual attack. I see this neighborhood where You have placed me as a training ground. "Be self-controlled and alert. Your enemy the devil prowls around like a roaring lion looking for someone to devour. Resist him, standing firm in the faith, because you know that your brothers throughout the world are undergoing the same kind of sufferings" (1 Pet. 5:8-9 NIV). You are training me, Lord, in my physical environment to be sensitive and alert to evil so I can recognize it in the spiritual realm and defend against both. Thank You, Lord.

September 25, 2008

"Set apart" to be sanctified. Lord, I have been reading WALKING WITH GOD by John Eldridge and tonight I was struck with remorse over the loss of a large part of my life, a loss which has ramifications in the present and future because of the way I chose to live for so long outside of Your will and blessing. Here I am going on forty-five years of age—I never married nor had children. I am now relocated to D.C. where I know practically nobody and am living alone in a condo with my dog. I feel isolated and my friends from West Virginia are not calling as much; the ties are becoming thin. I have more and more of a desire to be in Your Word and closer to You.

I am finding that I am repulsed by the things of this world—everything I see on television, no matter how innocent it might have seemed to me in the past, now bothers me because it is in direct violation of Your Word and Your ways. Lord, You have so completely transformed my life that the ways of this world are repulsive to me. I need more of You, Lord; I want to see people through Your eyes because I am having trouble with that right now, Lord. I pray that You continue to transform my life into the image of Your Son.

October 10, 2008

God, I feel so alone! I can't hear Your voice and I don't know why You asked me to move here. Did I hear You wrong? I did what I thought You wanted me to do and yet I am getting no direction! I feel abandoned! I want and need friends here but can't get over my fear and insecurity to go where I can meet people because I don't know how to be social. Please help me overcome this irrational fear—what is wrong with me? I can't seem to find a church I feel comfortable at. God, I want to hear Your voice and feel Your presence again! I need Your direction; show me why I am here, please! Don't abandon me here, God. Lead me to my new church home—get me connected to a body of believers. I feel as though I am separated from the flock and can't find my way back. Come find me, Lord!

"LORD, YOU HAVE SO COMPLETELY TRANSFORMED MY LIFE THAT THE WAYS OF THIS WORLD ARE REPULSIVE TO ME."

October 12, 2008

Lord, thank You for speaking to me today. This morning I asked You what church I should go to and You led me to Metropolitan Baptist. They had a guest speaker today who was used by You to speak directly to my heart! You confirmed for me that You and You alone have opened these doors for me. I have obediently walked through them and the enemy of my soul is therefore attacking me. The scripture reference for the message this morning was First Corinthians 16:5-9 where Paul is allowing You to direct his path even though he has his own plans. The preacher especially focused on this verse:

"Because a great door for effective work has opened to me, and there are many who oppose me" (NIV). I see clearly now that Satan is trying to destroy my destiny. Praise You, Lord God of the heavens. I stand firm in my faith that You will guide and direct my path to line up with Your will so long as I submit my spirit and my will to You every moment of every day. I commit to total surrender, Lord.

October 23, 2008

Lord, I thank You for drawing close to me as I seek a deeper and more intimate relationship with You. I have been asking You to show me what You would like to say by directing me to specific scriptures. Yesterday You had me read Revelation 4 where I saw Your holiness, and today You directed me to Psalm 46 where I was reminded about the words You spoke to me in Florida so many years ago: "Be still, and know that I am God" (Ps. 46:10a NIV).

I desire deep intimacy with You, Lord. You are the lover of my soul and I want to know You as intimately as You know me. I vow to hold nothing back from You, Lord; You can see all of me. I will reveal everything to You and ask for forgiveness of my sins. Wash me with Your blood, shine Your light into every corner of my being and burn away every impurity. I want to serve You with every fiber of my being. I love You, Lord, as much as a human can love the God of the universe. Please continue to reveal Yourself to me through Your Word and Your Spirit. Holy Spirit, fill me to overflowing and intercede on my behalf as I desire to connect with God. May my life have maximum impact for Your kingdom, Lord. Equip me for Your kingdom work.

November 9, 2008

Lord, thank You for Your touch this evening. Thank You, Holy Spirit, for loosing my tongue to pray in the spirit. God, I feel You healing deep wounds in my soul. I need Your intimacy; I need Your love; I need You to overshadow my soul, to cleanse me with Your fire—to burn away the dross and refine my heart. Thank You, Holy Spirit, for interceding and bringing healing to areas of my soul I can't even identify or think about. Thank You for loosing my tongue to cry out to my God for healing, deliverance and restoration. May You give me a thousand tongues to praise His holy name! I want to see Your face, God—I want to gaze into Your eyes and express my love for You. Allow me a glimpse into the spiritual realm; teach me, mold me and use all of me, God. I surrender everything I am to You for Your glory. Please, Lord, use me—use my life to make a difference in Your kingdom. I will do anything for You, Lord.

November 15, 2008

Lord, in my prayer time with You last night You revealed to me the wisdom in all You have worked out for me in this move to D.C. You have allowed the stripping away of so much that hindered my pure worship of You. All of the responsibility in maintaining ten acres and all of the time commuting back and forth to work and school was wearing on me, along with all of the responsibilities I had at church. All of this was taking away from my time with You. I thank You for all of Your blessings, in increasing my financial stability and ability to sow into the kingdom and my ability to spend more time with You in praise and worship and study of Your Word. I thank You for teaching me and healing me in so many ways. I thank You for increasing my faith and answering my prayers for deeper intimacy with You. I thank You for the churches I have been visiting; I plan to go to First Baptist Church of Glenarden tomorrow in search of my new church home. Direct me, Lord. Holy Spirit, cover me and overshadow me. Hover over me, consume me, take over my life; I give You all that I am and all that I ever hope to be. Consume in me all that is not of You—burn away all impurities in my life. I desire to give up all of me to You for Your glory. I no longer claim ownership of my life or my destiny. I completely surrender to You, Lord. I have such an incredible burning desire to experience all of You, God. I can't articulate my desire for You or my love for You. I am obsessed with Your presence. You are my heart's desire.

November 10, 2008

God, You never cease to amaze me! I am in awe of You again today. I went to the First Baptist Church of Glenarden this morning as You impressed upon my heart last night. Today was the church's 91st anniversary and there was a guest preacher: Pastor Maurice Watson from Macon, Georgia—the very same man I heard speak at the Metropolitan Baptist Church on October 12! He preached the exact same message from First Corinthians 16:9 that was so powerful to me six weeks ago! I thank You for Your Word and wait expectantly for what You have in store for me to glorify You, God. I love You, Lord, beyond words. I want such a deeper intimacy with You—teach me, Lord. Draw me close to You, for nothing else matters to me.

December 28, 2008

Lord, I thank You for my new church home! I am amazed that You led me to such a wonderful church with such a wonderful pastor: John K. Jenkins, Sr. I am so blessed by You to be where You have placed me, Lord! You are pouring into me mightily through Your powerful preacher. Thank You for what You are teaching me in preparation for what You want me to do; You are grooming me to serve You and Your kingdom. I have been reading over my past journals like I do at the end of each year to be reminded of Your power and majesty and Your powerful works in my life! I can hardly take it all in as I see Your mercy and grace and powerful hand at work so magnificently over these past five years!

November 23, 2003—I accepted You as Lord and Savior of my life; You have been working powerfully in and through me ever since. God, I give You all of my life. My life is not my own—every breath You allow me to breathe on this earth comes directly from You. May Your praise ever be on my lips and flowing from my heart right back to You, God. I love You more than I can describe in words and I live only to serve You. God, I pray for Your wisdom and discernment to walk through the doors You open for me with boldness and no fear. Guide and direct my every step, thought and action. Show me how I am to serve You in my new church home. May my life and service be a blessing to You, my Lord and my God. Empower me to be a bold witness for You, Lord!

"EMPOWER ME TO BE A BOLD WITNESS FOR YOU, LORD!"

I became a member of the First Baptist Church of Glenarden (FBCG) on January 25, 2009. I am so grateful that God planted me in this amazing church under the strong leadership of Pastor Jenkins, an incredible pastor who is a man after God's own heart and who has a passion for leading people to Christ and developing them into "dynamic disciples." I have experienced amazing spiritual growth under the leadership and teachings of FBCG and, in 2010, I began my training to become a minister. I have been given the opportunity to develop a ministry at FBCG to help others find freedom from the stronghold of same-sex attraction in their lives, and to educate parents, teachers, ministers and family members about the causes and healing of same-sex attraction. My purpose in life is to continue to share the incredible miracles that God has performed in my life and to live my life transparently so others will be drawn to Him.

My life experiences have enabled me to see how the church can and should react to people whom God is drawing into the church for healing.

We have an opportunity to demonstrate the love of Christ to people who are struggling with all areas of sin in their lives. We do this as Christians by allowing God to pour out His unconditional love on us so it can flow out of us to the people God places in our path. It is the Holy Spirit's job to convict people of sin. It is our job to love them unconditionally as Christ has loved us. Our job is to exemplify the love of Christ and, by doing that, to draw people to Jesus, teaching them to know Him and to love Him.

In the spring of 2009, I graduated from law school with honors. God is amazing! If you recall, I took the entrance exams for law school twice because I didn't have a high enough score to get accepted into law school according to the standards set by law schools in the area, but God enabled me to graduate near the top of my class! I had planned to take the bar exam that summer; however, I was called back to work at NOAA immediately following graduation and therefore had to postpone taking the bar exam until February 2010. Despite the setback, I ended up passing the test the first time I took it and I am now a licensed attorney.

You may be wondering what happened to Barb after I moved to D.C. She stayed in West Virginia, and we maintained a different kind of friendship for a number of years. That friendship was often rocky because it was difficult for us to figure out how to relate to each other as friends, having once been "married." We often had very different ideas about what that friendship should look like. You have to understand that when two people enter into a physical relationship, coupled with love, there are soul ties that are very difficult to sever. We have an incredible history together as God worked through both of us to deliver and heal each of us individually, and I thank God for bringing her into my life at the perfect time. It is not always easy to follow the will of God for your life. It took time for Him to reveal His truth to us, and He was exceedingly patient with us as I now believe we sometimes misunderstood what He was communicating to us. He also never moved too fast for us. He took His time and put people and circumstances in our path until His perfect will was fully revealed to us. He then carried both of us through the emotional and painful transition from homosexuality to healing.

I have been completely transformed and healed from my same-sex attraction. I no longer have any interest in physical or emotional relationships with women and instead have learned how to have healthy non-sexual relationships with women. This was brought about through the loving care of women of God who were willing to spend the time with me that I needed for healing. I am now physically attracted to men, and I pray that God will bring a man into my life to marry someday soon so I can experience what God's perfect will is for human companionship and sexuality.

I am excited about what God is doing in my life and I continue to dig into and study the Word of God every day for the deep riches of wisdom and understanding that God reveals to each one of His children who desire to know Him. It is my heart's desire to spend the rest of my life helping others find Jesus and the same healing He established for me.

"And the Lord said, '[Debora, Debora]! Indeed, Satan has asked for you, that he may sift you as wheat. But I have prayed for you, that your faith should not fail; and when you have returned to Me, strengthen Your brethren'" (Luke 22:31-32).

My Prayer for You

Father, I pray for Your blessing over the life of the person holding this book. I pray that You will stir the person's spirit and draw him or her to You if this reader has not yet yielded his or her heart to You and invited You to be Lord and Savior of his or her life. Do not let this person rest easy until he or she has made the only decision that will change his or her eternal destiny!

For the reader who already knows You and has committed his or her life to You, I pray that You will give this person an unquenchable desire to dig into the deep riches of Your Word and that You will show this individual his or her own life in the pages of the Bible. Transform the life of the person holding this book; show Yourself mighty and strong in his or her life; bring healing, deliverance and peace; and give this person a boldness to share the testimony of his or her life with the world so all will know Your power and presence is strong in the lives of Your people today.

Finally, I pray God will "grant you, according to the riches of His glory, to be strengthened with might through His Spirit in the inner man, that Christ may dwell in your hearts through faith; that you, being rooted and grounded in love, may be able to comprehend with all the saints what is the width and length and depth and height—to know the love of Christ which passes knowledge; that you may be filled with all the fullness of God," amen (Eph. 3:16-19).

About the Author

Debora was a self-proclaimed atheist, fully entrenched in her homosexual life and gay community when God began to work on her heart in late 1994. Nine years later, in November, 2003, she surrendered her life to Jesus Christ and began to read the Bible every day because she wanted to know more about the God who had drawn her back to Himself. Through His Word - God revealed the truth about how He wanted her to live her life, and in January 2006, she turned away from 18 years of living as a lesbian. She experienced inner healing from the wounds that propelled her into lesbianism with the support of a group of loving women at her church who invested in her life and loved her unconditionally. She now facilitates a Bible Study at her church to help women who struggle with unwanted Same-Sex Attraction (SSA) to understand the causes and healing of SSA by searching the Word of God.

Debora is the co-author (with James E. Phelan) of *Practical Exercises For Women In Recovery Of Same Sex Attraction*. She has a passion for teaching, speaking, and writing about SSA to better equip churches to make those who experience SSA feel welcome so they too can experience the unconditional love and healing of Jesus Christ. She Loves the Lord with all her heart and desires to help people completely transform their lives through their personal relationship with Jesus.

Contact the author via
Email: DBarrMinistries@gmail.com
Web Site: DBarrMinistries.Org